OPIE MACLEOD

Jediism Explained

Contents

Acknowledgments

This Book is Dedicated to Dennis Blundell.

Retired California Highway Patrol. Loving Father. Devoted Husband.

I have spent over half my life looking for my Yoda. Or really any father-figure that would have uplifted and taught me things about life. Fortunately in my adult years I got a step-dad that stepped up (as the silly t-shirt goes). He spoke at my wedding. He always encouraged and supported me in the pursuit of my dreams. He had good questions. Kept me grounded. Taught me the value of financial and social wellness and the balance with each other. More importantly he taught me the value of just being a good and honest person. He wasn't a saint, wasn't perfect, but he was real, caring, and willing to learn/grow. Generous and kind with a great sense of humor, he would have made a great Jedi Master. I will cherish the memories and miss not making new ones. Love You Dad.

Introduction

Introduction: What Is This Path?

Welcome, dear Jedi — or simply curious seeker flipping through these pages. If you're previewing this book, thank you for giving me these precious seconds of your attention. Let's make them count.

In short, this book is an exploration of the **Jedi lifestyle**, often referred to as *Jediism*. That word — Jediism — tends to raise eyebrows. But here's what it really means:

> ***Being a Jedi means living a life of world-betterment through self-betterment — wrapped in Star Wars inspiration.***

We understand Star Wars is fiction. Yoda isn't real. There's no secret Jedi Temple hidden in the mountains (that we're telling you about, anyway). But the *ideals*? The values? The practices? Very real. Very useful. And very needed.

Concepts like **peace**, **knowledge**, **serenity**, and **harmony** are not fantasy. They're found in nearly every wisdom tradition. Practices such as **meditation**, **physical wellness**, **conflict resolution**, and **self-discipline** are grounded tools for real life. Even the most mystical-sounding element — the *Force* — can be understood in ways that are both philosophical and practical, whether viewed metaphorically, spiritually, or even psychologically.

What You'll Find in This Book

Here's what's inside:

- **A Brief History**: We'll look at how modern-day Jedi communities came to be, how Jediism emerged as a term, and what it means today.
- **A Glimpse at the Variants**: Jedi Realism, Jedi Pragmatism, Jedi Philosophy — different paths, different tones, same core: living by the Jedi virtues.
- **Jedi Groups & Movements**: A tour through communities that have kept this path alive, from solo practitioners to online academies to nonprofit organizations.
- **The Philosophy in Practice**: We'll explore the ideals of the Jedi Path — how they're expressed, where they came from, and how they're being lived today. You'll also find resources to explore deeper on your own.
- **A Beginner's Course**: You'll be guided through foundational training — meditations, physical practices, and reflections — designed to help you *live* as a Jedi. Completing this doesn't make you a Jedi Knight. But it does help you start walking the path.
- **Answers to the FAQs**: What about Jedi Temples? Robes? The Dark Side? We'll cover the common questions — not to dictate what's "right," but to offer perspective, clarity, and grounded practices.

Let's be clear: Jediism is not the Jedi Order from Star Wars. We aren't space monks with laser swords. We're real people, inspired by those stories, trying to live with purpose, clarity, and compassion. We're not cosplaying belief systems. We're applying them.

If you're curious about what it means to live as a Jedi in the real world, you're in the right place.

Reflection & Practice: Start Where You Are

Journal Prompt

- What brought you to this book? Curiosity? Conflict? The Force?
- What do you already believe about the Jedi Path? What questions are you carrying?

Daily Practice

- Take a few deep breaths. Place a hand over your heart. Say quietly: *"I am here to learn. I am open to growth."* That's all it takes to begin.

APBP Test

Is this book Applicable, Practical, Beneficial, and Positive for your life?
   (We'll be using that test throughout the journey.)

Ready to step into a larger world?
   Let's begin.

Introduction to the Author

Now that we've covered what this book is about, it's probably a good idea to tell you who's doing all the blah-blah-blah-ing.

My name is **Kevin** — though most in the Jedi community know me as **Opie**

Macleod. I've been involved in this path since around 1997. Technically, I could stretch that to 1995, but honestly, the Jedi community back then was a chaotic mess of scattered forum posts and fan pages. So let's just say: I've been around a while. Since *before* the term *Jediism* was even a thing.

In 2007, I founded what would become **Jedi Living** — a community and website focused on turning Jedi philosophy into real-world practice. Over the years, I've been called things like **Administrator**, **Councilor**, **Knight**, and even **Master**. Do those titles matter? Not really. But people tend to feel more comfortable when the person offering guidance has at least been around the metaphorical (or literal) Temple a few times.

I've written and taught over **200 Jedi lessons** (with quite a few still in active use), created hundreds of videos on Jedi topics for YouTube, and built multiple Jedi training programs — both online and offline. I've majored in philosophy, graduated a police academy, and generally devoted the past two decades to testing, refining, and living the Jedi path.

But if you're looking for a formal resume with a degree in English Literature or professional writing experience — I don't have that. So yes, expect a few grammatical hiccups and a casual, sometimes self-deprecating tone. I write the way I talk: conversational, a little nerdy, and occasionally sarcastic.

What you'll find in this book is drawn from **experience** — not theory. From personal failures and insights. From community trial and error. From watching Jedi groups rise, fall, evolve, and find meaning. My writing might not win awards, but it's honest. And more importantly, it's usable.

> *I don't claim to be the Jedi authority. I'm just someone who's walked the path long enough to point out the potholes and shortcuts.*

If this book speaks to you — if the practices and philosophy feel beneficial to your life — then great. Use it. Question it. Test it. Apply it. And if it doesn't resonate? That's fine too. There are many paths, and not all are meant to be walked by everyone.

What matters most is this: **From this point on, you are your own Jedi Master.**

I can share what I've learned, but it's *your* path to walk.

Workbook Companion: Know Your Guide — Know Yourself

Reflection Prompt

- What qualities do you seek in a mentor or guide?
- Are you open to learning from someone imperfect but experienced?

Journal Inquiry

- What would your own Jedi introduction sound like?
- Try writing 3–5 sentences that describe your relationship with the Jedi path — real or aspirational.

Daily Practice

- Say aloud: *"I walk my own path. But I am never alone in the journey."*

Optional Mission

- Check out a few Jedi Living videos on YouTube. See if you connect with the content or presentation.
- *(Search: Jedi Living – Opie Macleod)*

1

History of the Jedi Community

The Shortest History Lesson Possible

To understand where the Jedi Path begins, we must travel back — not to ancient Japan or medieval Europe — but to the year **1977**.

Now, some folks will tell you the Jedi were inspired by the **samurai traditions** of feudal Japan. Others will point to the **Knights Templar** of medieval times. Some will reach further back into the roots of **Stoicism**, while others will align Jedi ideals with **Taoism** from ancient China. And many will name-drop **Joseph Campbell** and the **monomyth** — the "hero's journey" as the spiritual DNA behind Jediism.

And they're not wrong. These influences are real and worth exploring. It's inspiring to see how Jediism shares common themes with established traditions: discipline, honor, purpose, harmony, and service. But shared ideals don't make them the same path. Inspiration isn't duplication.

🔥 *The Spark: George Lucas and the Jedi Blueprint*

George Lucas created Star Wars — and with it, the Jedi — over the course of many years. His inspirations ranged from *Flash Gordon* and *Buck Rogers* to samurai films like *The Hidden Fortress*. Some speculate that the term "Jedi" was inspired by *Jidai-geki* (period dramas), though Lucas has never confirmed that.

What he has confirmed is that he was heavily influenced by **Joseph Campbell's** *The Hero with a Thousand Faces*. The idea of the archetypal hero — the one who answers a call, undergoes transformation, and returns to serve others — was embedded in the Jedi narrative.

But again, these influences alone didn't create *Jediism*. Just as fire needs more than a single spark, the Jedi Community needed more than just stories.

The Fire Triangle: How the Community Truly Began

To understand how the Jedi community was born, I like to use a simple analogy: **fire**.

For a fire to ignite, it needs:

- **Fuel** – Something to burn
- **Oxygen** – Something to breathe
- **Ignition** – A spark to start it

Let's apply this to the Jedi path.

Fuel: Star Wars and the Dream of the Jedi

By the 1980s and early 90s, *Star Wars* had been inspiring people for years. Some fans quietly tried to live by Jedi ideals, often blending practices from **Buddhism**, **Taoism**, **Stoicism**, and **Yoga** into their daily lives. But these were isolated journeys — individual flames flickering alone. There were no real gathering places, no defined movement, no common identity beyond fandom.

Still, Star Wars was the necessary *fuel*. Without it, the idea of real-world

Jedi wouldn't exist.

Oxygen: The Rise of the Internet (1995–1997)

By **1995,** the internet was becoming more accessible. **Windows 95** launched, making computers more user-friendly. People began creating personal websites and connecting through online forums and chatrooms.

Among the earliest fan sites was **Jason Ruspini's Star Wars Home Page** (1994).

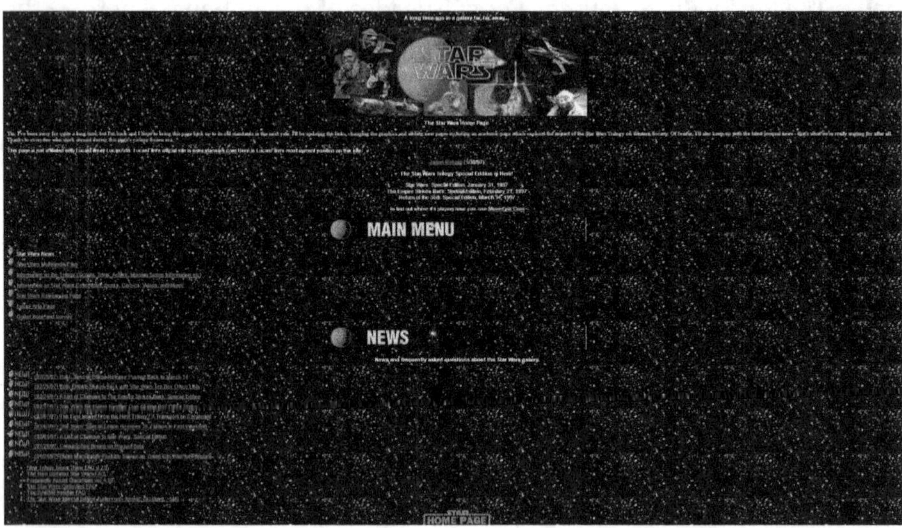

Soon, many Star Wars chatrooms and "Mos Eisley Cantina" sites began popping up. These were the first digital taverns — communities where early Jedi thinkers met, argued, and dreamed.

This was the **oxygen**. The internet allowed isolated fans to find each other. To organize. To speak a common language. To ask a now-legendary question:

Why can't I live as a Jedi?

Ignition: The Return of Star Wars (1997)

The **Special Edition** re-releases of the original Star Wars trilogy hit theaters in 1997, reigniting public interest. A new generation (my generation) got to experience Star Wars on the big screen. Then came the whispers of *The Phantom Menace.* Suddenly, Star Wars was back.

And people weren't just excited for the movies. Some of us were hungry for *meaning.* We wanted to embody the Jedi ideals. Not cosplay them. *Live* them.

This was the **spark**. And it lit the flame.

The First Jedi Websites

Two of the earliest websites to focus on real-world Jedi philosophy were:

- **Star Wars: The Jedi Academy** (also called the Jedi Praxeum on Yavin IV)

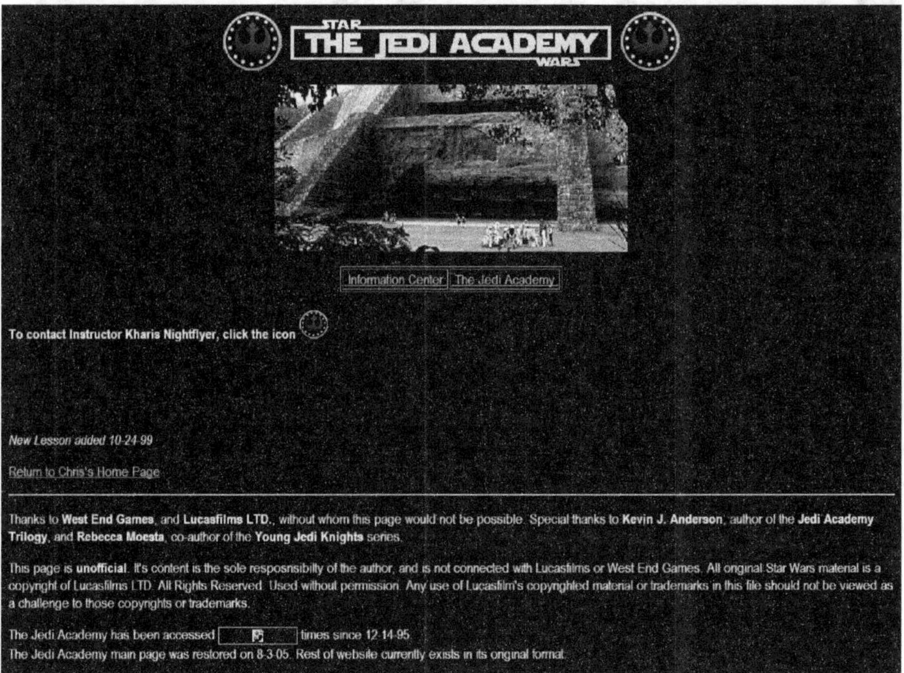

- **Jedi Lore**

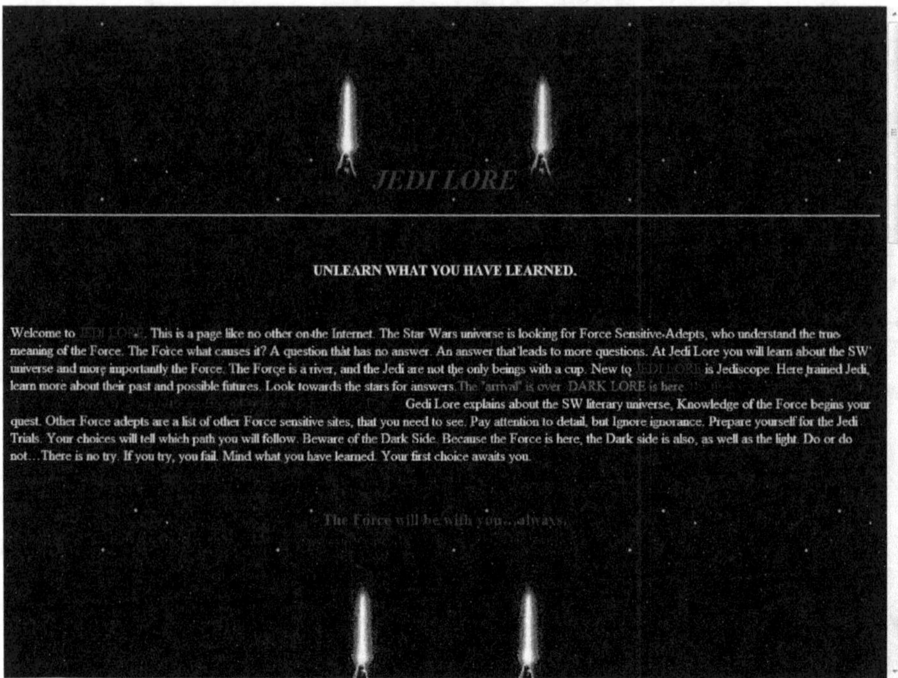

Though limited in interactivity (no forums or email groups), these sites planted the seed: *Maybe this could be something more.*

When *The Phantom Menace* released in **1999**, the fire spread fast. Five new Jedi groups emerged:

- **The Jedi Academy**
- **The Force Academy**
- **The Jedi Creed**
- **The Jedi Temple** (pictured below)
- **The Jedi of the New Millennium**

These weren't just fan or role-playing sites (though elements of both existed). They were focused on **living the Jedi life** — embracing the philosophy, practicing the virtues, and bringing Jedi ideals into the real world.

By the summer of 1999, the **Jedi Community** had become a thing unto itself. Not a fandom. Not a religion (yet). Not a role-play. But a living, evolving lifestyle. Personal Note: This why I often state my Jedi start date in 1999, simply because before that it wasn't really a Community to belong to.

And it only grew from there.

Workbook Companion: Origins of a Path

Journal Prompt

- What were your first experiences with Star Wars or the Jedi?
- When did you first consider the idea of living like a Jedi?

Discussion Prompt

- What do you think makes a belief system or philosophy "real"?
- Is it enough for something to be meaningful, or does it need structure,

history, or legitimacy?

Practice

- Explore an origin story — not of the Jedi, but of *you*.

    Where did your desire for personal growth begin?
        What stories, mentors, or events inspired your path?

Optional Mission

- Use the APBP Test on the Jedi Path origin story:

    *Is it **Applicable** to your life?*
        *Is it **Practical** to live by?*
        *Is it **Beneficial** to your well-being?*
        *Is it **Positive** in how it shapes your view of the world?*

History of the Terminology

I could write an entire book just on the history of the Jedi Community — especially the rise and fall of the Five Giants. The personalities, the politics, the flame wars, the forum crashes. It'd be a *Game of Thrones* saga, only with robes, forum ranks, and a lot more meditation.

But for now, we'll keep it focused.

One key question almost every real-world Jedi faces at some point is:

   Where did the word "Jediism" come from?

Let's break it down.

The Word Before the Word

Was "Jediism" coined back in **1977** to mirror Buddhism or Taoism? Maybe. But if it was, it didn't stick. From **1995 to 2000**, during the earliest days of the online Jedi movement, *no one* used the word Jediism. We simply called ourselves Jedi. We were building a way of life, not naming a religion.

The word "Jediism" didn't appear until a strange alignment of elements in **2001** — and, like so many things in modern culture, it started as a **joke**.

The 2001 Census Spark

In 2001, people in **the United Kingdom, New Zealand, and Australia** received an email that essentially said:

> "If enough people list 'Jedi' as their religion on the census, the government will have to recognize it as an official religion!"

This was false. Classic internet-era fake news. But it caught fire.

People listed Jedi as their religion for a variety of reasons:

- Some thought it was funny
- Some were making a protest statement
- Some were fans who genuinely felt Star Wars reflected their spiritual worldview
- Some were sincerely trying to live as Jedi in real life

And the **media loved it**.

News outlets around the world covered the story. And they used a brand-new word to describe it:

Jediism.

That was the first time many of us heard the term.

Collision Course: Jediism Meets the Community

There were no "Jediism" websites at the time. The active Jedi communities had been evolving quietly, refining practices and philosophies for years. But when newly inspired people searched for *Jediism* online, they didn't find us. So many of them created new websites and groups from scratch — unknowingly reinventing the wheel.

Meanwhile, the established Jedi groups watched this new wave arrive... with mixed feelings.

Some saw potential. Others saw regression.

They had worked through years of trial-and-error, conflict mediation, and forum drama. Now here were the "Jediism" newcomers — full of enthusiasm, but unaware of the history and lessons already earned.

This caused a split.

A look at the difference between community-evolved sites and the new Jediism efforts in 2001:

JEDI – A Jedi Realist website created by Relan Volkum and Streen, 2001.

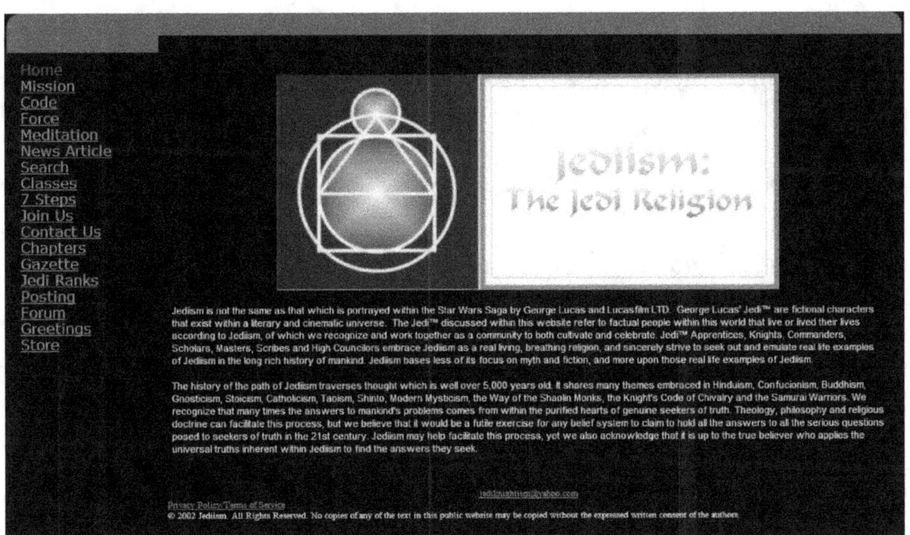

Jediism – 2002 Website created by Chris Chandra

Jediism vs. Jedi Realism

As the term *Jediism* gained traction in the media, some groups tried to distance themselves from it. They didn't like being associated with what they saw as a media stunt or a shallow expression of the path.

Thus, the label **Jedi Realism** was born — meant to distinguish those who saw the Jedi Path not as a religion, but as a lifestyle, philosophy, or personal code.

- **Jedi Realists** accused Jediism groups of chasing tax-exempt status and failing to honor the depth of the path.
- **Jediism adherents** accused Jedi Realists of being fence-sitters, unwilling to truly commit to Jedi as a spiritual path.

Lines were drawn. Forums split. New sites and groups emerged. "Ism" wars began.

But the truth?

We were all still just people trying to be Jedi — we just had different language, goals, and approaches.

Bridging the Divide

Over time, things calmed. As the community matured, so did the understanding that terminology wasn't the core issue — practice was.

Yes, the **Temple of the Jedi Order** (TOTJO) gained 501(c)(3) religious non-profit status in the United States. Yes, the **United Kingdom rejected Jediism** as a religion in 2016. These were milestones, but they didn't define the whole path.

Many groups still identify by their "ism":

- **Church of Jediism**
- **Institute for Jedi Realist Studies**

But the larger community now tends to favor simpler terms:

"I'm a Jedi. I live the Jedi Path."

Religion or not — that's up to you. Labels are useful until they get in the way. Your actions matter far more than your taxonomy.

Workbook Companion: Your Jedi Language

Reflection Prompt

- Which term feels most aligned with your path: *Jedi, Jediist, Jedi Realist, Jedi Pragmatist, none of the above? Why?*

Journal Exercise

- Describe the "vibe" of each term for you. How do you respond to each? Does one inspire you more than the others?
- *Jedi*
- *Jediism*
- *Jedi Realism*
- *Jedi Philosophy*
- *The Jedi Way*

Daily Practice

- Say aloud:

  "I am not bound by labels. I am defined by how I live."

Optional Mission

- Try explaining your take on the Jedi path to a friend *without* using the word "Jedi." What values or practices remain when the label is removed?

2

Jedi Philosophy

Development of Jedi Philosophy

In the early days of the Jedi Community, there wasn't much "Jedi Philosophy" to work with.

Sure, we had the wise quips from **Yoda**, **Obi-Wan**, and the occasional gem from the *Expanded Universe*. But in truth, the mid-to-late '90s were still pretty sparse in terms of philosophical groundwork. So what did we do?

We filled in the gaps — often with pre-existing traditions.

Buddhism. Taoism. Stoicism. Yoga. Even bits of Western philosophy. The result? **A lot of thoughtful exploration**, but not a lot of original growth. Jedi groups often leaned so heavily into other traditions that the Jedi path became a collage rather than a coherent structure.

This wasn't a bad thing. It was a **natural starting point**. But it did create a sort of stagnation — a philosophical identity crisis. We had the **inspiration**, but not yet a unified method of *application*.

The Jedi Code: A Spark of Original Thought

The one foundational text we *did* have was the **Jedi Code** — a four-line mantra originally written by **Greg Costikyan** in 1987 for the *West End Games Star Wars Roleplaying Game*:

> *There is no emotion; there is peace.*
>> *There is no ignorance; there is knowledge.*
>> *There is no passion; there is serenity.*
>> *There is no death; there is the Force.*

It was never intended to be a real-life moral code. It was a tool for roleplayers. But it resonated — deeply. It gave us something to hold onto. Something that *felt* true.

Interestingly, the Jedi Code is thought to be loosely inspired by the **Heart Sutra** of Mahāyāna Buddhism, which includes lines like:

> *There is no ignorance,*
>> *and no end to ignorance.*
>> *There is no old age and death,*
>> *and no end to old age and death...*

So naturally, early Jedi spent more time studying **Eastern philosophy** than the fictional Jedi path itself.

But eventually, we started asking new questions:

> *What if the fiction was enough?*
>> *What if we could extract meaningful, practical wisdom directly from Star Wars?*

The APBP Test: Filtering Fiction for Wisdom

At **Jedi Living**, we began using a tool called the **APBP Test** — a framework for deciding whether a Jedi idea (from any source) is worth applying:

- **Applicable** – Can I apply this to my life?
- **Practical** – Can I live by this realistically?
- **Beneficial** – Does this bring improvement or growth?
- **Positive** – Does this lead to better outcomes for me and others?

Let's try it out. Here's how we broke down the Jedi Code — line by line — and developed **living philosophy** from the fiction.

Line One: There is no emotion; there is peace.

Literal interpretation? Doesn't pass the APBP Test.
  We *do* have emotions. Denying that is neither healthy nor wise.
  But if we interpret this as:

"Don't let your emotions control your decisions,"

...then we're onto something.
  Yoda warned Luke on Dagobah:

"Anger, fear, aggression... the dark side of the Force are they."

Unchecked emotions lead to imbalance. And most of us have made bad decisions in emotional spirals — angry texts, regretful words, impulsive actions. We've *lived* this.

Peace, then, isn't the absence of emotion — it's the ability to navigate emotion with clarity.

APBP Verdict: ✓ Yes. When interpreted metaphorically, this line passes.

Line Two: *There is no ignorance; there is knowledge.*

Again, literally? Not so much. Ignorance is very real — just ask my grammar.

But what's being *suggested* here is that we strive to overcome ignorance. To pursue understanding. Luke's entire journey in the Original Trilogy is a path from *assumption* to *awareness*.

> *"A Jedi uses the Force for knowledge and defense, never for attack."* — Yoda

Knowledge, practice, growth — these are our antidotes to ignorance.

APBP Verdict: ✓ Yes, when interpreted as an aspiration to remain teachable.

Line Three: *There is no passion; there is serenity.*

This one throws a lot of people off. Isn't passion good? Doesn't it drive creativity, purpose, even love?

Yes — but not when it becomes obsession or recklessness. Passion without grounding becomes imbalance.

Yoda's critique of Luke:

> *"All his life has he looked away... to the future, to the horizon. Never his mind on where he was."*

Serenity, then, isn't the rejection of passion. It's *balance* — the ability to channel energy without losing presence.

APBP Verdict: ✓ Yes. Passion with mindfulness creates serenity.

Line Four: There is no death; there is the Force.

At first glance, this seems to imply some mystical afterlife — force ghosts and blue glows.

But it's more than that. Think of Yoda's final wisdom:

> *"Twilight is upon me, and soon night must fall. That is the way of things. The way of the Force."*

Death is a **part of life**. Not something to fear — but to understand. To accept. To integrate into our worldview as natural.

> *The Jedi Code here offers comfort, not denial.*

APBP Verdict: ✓ Yes. A poetic reminder of impermanence and presence.

The "Yet" Version: A Modern Adaptation

In 1996, the Code evolved into a more nuanced version — commonly called the "Yet Code." It goes like this:

> *Emotion, yet peace.*
> *Ignorance, yet knowledge.*
> *Passion, yet serenity.*
> *Chaos, yet harmony.*
> *Death, yet the Force.*

This version better reflects **real-life Jedi practice**. It acknowledges the presence of these forces in our lives — and offers a path to navigate them.

From Fiction to Philosophy

This process — of **extracting insight**, testing it, applying it, and refining it — is how real-world Jedi philosophy developed.

It started with inspiration.

It grew through experimentation.

It matured through practice.

The Jedi Code may have been born from fiction. But we made it **real** through **action**, **reflection**, and **adaptation**.

> *Jedi Philosophy isn't a set of rigid beliefs. It's a living path. A practice. A compass. A choice.*

Workbook Companion: Your Jedi Philosophy

Journal Prompts

- Which version of the Jedi Code resonates more with you — the original or the "Yet" version? Why?
- What fictional quotes or concepts have shaped your real-life beliefs?
- How do you personally define "serenity"?

Daily Practice

- Choose one line from the Jedi Code.
- Repeat it silently in meditation.
- Reflect on how it shows up (or doesn't) in your daily life.
- Ask yourself: Does this line pass the APBP test *for me*?

Guided Exercise: The APBP Test

> *Pick your favorite Jedi quote from any source — a movie, novel, game, or show.*

Put it to the test:

- Is it **Applicable** to your daily life?
- Is it **Practical** to live by?
- Is it **Beneficial** to your well-being?
- Is it **Positive** in how it affects others?

If it passes — **use it**. Let it guide you. If it doesn't — **release it**. Not all inspiration translates into action.

The Core of Jediism

The **core of Jediism** isn't found in a single sacred book or absolute doctrine.

It's found in the living, evolving texts written by real Jedi — for real Jedi.

Some of these writings draw directly from our fictional inspiration. Others are rooted in ancient traditions like the **Code of Chivalry**, penned by the **Duke of Burgundy**. And still others come straight from personal, hard-earned experience — from Jedi walking the path every day in real life.

There's no *one* definitive text. No single "Jedi Bible."

Different groups use different sources depending on what resonates with them, what works, and what they've tested over time.

Core Texts of the Community

Here's a quick overview of where the main schools tend to lean:

- **Jedi Living** focuses on:
- The **Jedi Circle**
- The **Jedi Precepts**
- The **Jedi Method**
- **Temple of the Jedi Order (TOTJO)** tends to favor:
- The **21 Jedi Maxims**
- The **16 Teachings of the Jedi**
- **Temple of the Jedi Force** (and others) also use:
- The **33 Teachings of the Jedi**

Each of these are available online, often free to read, download, or study. Many Jedi groups list them openly on their websites.

> *While the texts vary, the themes are remarkably consistent.*

Shared Ideals Across All Jedi Paths

Despite the differences in wording or structure, every core text points to similar foundational values:

- **Meditation** and attunement to the **Force**
- **Integrity, Accountability**, and **Responsibility**
- A commitment to **Continual Growth, Learning,** and **Training**
- A call to **serve** and **support others** along the path
- The importance of **Discipline** and **Commitment**
- The value of **Study** and pursuit of **Knowledge**
- An emphasis on **Defense**, especially protecting the vulnerable
- Shared virtues: **Service, Wellness, Peace, Harmony, Patience**
- Deep **Respect for Life** in all its forms

No matter where you go in the Jedi community — regardless of name, rank, or "ism" — these ideals will be expected of you. They form the **real heart of Jediism**.

You don't need to memorize every version of every creed. But you *do* need to understand the *spirit* of these texts — because that's what Jediism is built on.

A Note on Copyrights and Inclusion

You might wonder why I'm not laying out every one of these texts in full here.

It's simple: many of them were written by other Jedi authors, and I respect their ownership and effort. I was able to get permission to use them in The Situational Jedi book, so they are explored and listed there. But as I didn't get permission at the time of writing this book - they will not be included.

You can find them with a quick search — and I *encourage* you to do that. Read widely. Study different styles. Find what speaks to you.

But in this book, I'll be focusing on the pieces I *did* create — such as the **Jedi Circle**, the **Precepts**, and more — because I can legally and ethically include those in full.

The Universal Jedi Standard

Call it the Jedi Way. The Jedi Lifestyle. Jedi Realism. Jediism. Whatever label suits you.

What matters most is this:

> ***No matter what Jedi group you explore, the path will ask you to live with discipline, service, wisdom, peace, and presence.***

So let's not just read about these values.

Let's *train them.*

Workbook Companion: Identifying Your Jedi Core

Reflection Prompt

- Of the core ideals mentioned above, which one feels most natural to you? Which one feels like a challenge?
- What is one way you already live like a Jedi in your daily life?

Journal Exercise

- Choose *three* values from this list:
- Meditation
- Integrity
- Accountability
- Service
- Discipline
- Peace
- Respect for Life
- Knowledge
- For each, write:

1. What this ideal means to you.
2. A real-life example where you succeeded or struggled with it.
3. One way you could strengthen it in your life this week.

Daily Practice

- Recite this aloud (or in meditation):

"I commit to learning. I commit to service. I commit to the Jedi Way — not as belief, but as practice."

Ready for Jedi Training?

From this point on, the path becomes personal. We'll go beyond theory and into practice. You'll begin training not to *believe* in Jediism — but to **live it**.

So take a breath.

Turn the page.

Let's begin your training.

The Core of Our Training

Before we dive into the training content itself, let's address two important truths up front:

Limitation One: You Get What You Give

This isn't a magical book. It won't unlock mystical Jedi powers just by sitting on your shelf (though that would be nice). Like any path of growth, **you will only get out of it what you put in**.

You are — and always will be — **your own Jedi Master**.

This book isn't here to hand you your knighthood. It's here to give you a forge.

Limitation Two: This Is Not a Full Training Program

This book is a **summary and overview** of Jedi ideals, practices, and philosophy. It is not a structured, hands-on, accountability-driven training course. Think of this as your **foundation** — your starting platform.

If you're looking for a more formal or communal program, I recommend pairing this with an online training course (like those at Jedi Living or similar communities). But don't worry — you'll find plenty here to begin shaping your path.

The Forge: You Are the Lightsaber

Let's get metaphorical for a moment.

In the fictional Jedi tradition, the **lightsaber** is a symbol of:

- **Light** in the darkness
- **Skill** earned through discipline
- **Authority** earned through readiness

Jedi construct their lightsabers when they are ready — as a rite of passage. It's a reflection of who they are.

> *In the real world? You are the lightsaber.*

You are the tool. You are the instrument. You are the light in the shadows. And now, it's time to build yourself.

The Forge Process

Each Jedi begins with their own raw materials — the experiences, habits, knowledge, and scars you've picked up along your journey. Some are refined and useful. Others are warped or worn from hardship. Some may be entirely missing.

That's okay.

We're not forging perfection. We're forging presence, purpose, and practice.

As you read and reflect, you'll add to your materials.

As you practice and fail and try again, you'll refine your shape.

As you live the path, the heat of life will temper you.

The tools of the forge — your hammer, your anvil, the fire itself — will be:

- **Self-discipline**
- **Reflection**
- **Community**
- **Jedi philosophy**
- **The Force, however you define it**

Over time, you'll learn when to strike, when to rest, when to cool off, and when to return to the flame. This is the value of a Jedi community, online or offline — experienced Jedi can help guide the process. You don't have to figure it out alone.

Our Template: The Jedi Precepts

For this portion of the journey, we'll be using the **Jedi Precepts** as our training mold — a guide for the shape we're forging.

The Jedi Precepts were created in response to a request:

"How do we hold Jedi accountable to their ideals?"

Originally inspired by the *Rules of Behavior* from the *Power of the Jedi Sourcebook*, the Precepts were drafted to define what it meant to **live as a Jedi** within a specific community. After refinement in 2010, they became a practical and accessible blueprint — one we'll use throughout this course.

You don't have to adopt them word-for-word, but they provide a reliable, tested framework for Jedi living.

Take Your Time

There's no finish line here. Jedi training is not about rushing.

It's about **reflection**, **refinement**, and **real-life integration**.

This is a **journey**, not a checklist.

You don't become a Jedi by finishing this book.

You become a Jedi by living its lessons — slowly, consistently, intentionally.

Workbook Companion: Preparing for the Forge

Journal Prompt

- What raw materials are you bringing into your Jedi journey?

    (Think: values, strengths, flaws, patterns, experiences)

Reflection Prompt

- What part of you feels like it's "ready" to be forged?
- What part still feels uncertain or missing?

Daily Practice

- Begin a simple breath meditation:
- Sit comfortably.
- Inhale slowly through your nose (count of 4).
- Hold for 2 seconds.
- Exhale through your mouth (count of 6).
- Repeat for 5–10 minutes.
- As you breathe, quietly repeat:

"I am present. I am shaping. I am becoming."

Training Frame

- This section marks the beginning of your **Jedi Foundations**.
- You will be invited to:
- Read a Jedi concept
- Reflect and journal
- Apply a daily practice
- Track your own journey

Quote to Carry With You

"A Jedi must have the deepest commitment, the most serious mind."
— Yoda, The Empire Strikes Back

You ready?
Good.
Let's step into the forge.

3

Jedi Training - The Forge

Forging Process One: The Introduction

What We Are Not: Clearing the Impurities

You don't define something by what it's *not*.

But you *can* begin to shape something by **clearing away the misconceptions**.

If you're reading this, you already carry an image of what it means to be a Jedi. Some spark brought you here. Some idea. Some scene. Some ideal. And that's powerful — but often unexamined. Our first step, then, is like heating raw metal: we bring things to the surface.

Before we refine what it *means* to be a Jedi, let's briefly summarize the **core of the path**.

What Being a Jedi Does Mean

A **Jedi** is someone who seeks world-betterment through self-betterment, *using inspiration from Star Wars as a symbolic language to frame their journey.*

The structure we'll be using to shape this process is called the **Jedi Circle**. It includes:

Five Practices:

- Meditation
- Physical Fitness
- Diplomacy
- Awareness
- Self-Discipline

Five Tenets:

- Peace
- Knowledge
- Serenity
- Harmony
- The Force

Five Traits:

- Patience
- Empathy
- Equity
- Accountability
- Decorum

Five Values:

- Self-Honesty
- Gratitude
- Erudition
- Guidance
- Commitment

Five Goals:

- Proficiency
- Service
- Defense
- Create
- Discover

This gives us the rough outline of the Jedi form — the blade we're crafting in the forge. But to refine it, we need to confront what we *are not*.

Misconceptions to Remove from the Jedi Path

✕ *Jedi Are Not Star Wars Fanatics*

You don't need to know who directed *The Empire Strikes Back*.
   You don't need to memorize the Sith species from *Knights of the Old Republic*.
   You don't even have to *like* all of Star Wars.

Jediism is inspired by Star Wars — but it's not a fandom requirement.

You can love the fiction or just admire the values. Either way, Jediism is about how you live, not how much trivia you know.

✕ *Jedi Are Not Arrogant or Infallible*

Yes — believe in yourself.
   But no — don't assume you're above failure.
   Even Jedi Masters stumble. The difference is: they **learn**, **adapt**, and **take responsibility**.

Jedi confidence comes from clarity, not ego.

✕ *Jedi Are Not Invasive*

Curiosity is a virtue. Intrusion is not.
  The Jedi do not spy, snoop, or gossip under the banner of "learning."
  We seek **truth**, but we also respect **boundaries**.
  We ask questions — but we don't *pry.*

✕ *Jedi Are Not Defeatists*

We fail. We fall.
  But we rise again — that's the way of things.

  A Jedi may plan for setbacks, but never prepares to give up.

Luke's failure in the Dagobah swamp? It wasn't his power that failed.
  It was his *belief.*

✕ *Jedi Are Not Reckless*

Yes, we act — when the moment calls.
  But we do not leap without clarity.

  The Jedi train to know when to strike, and when to wait.
  When to speak, and when to remain silent.

✕ *Jedi Are Not Stubborn*

Tenacious? Yes.
  Closed-minded? No.
  We remain open to being wrong, to learning, to letting go.
  Anakin clung to control — and it destroyed him.
  A Jedi lets the Force *flow.*

✕ Jedi Do Not Wear Jedi Costumes in Daily Life

Uniforms are for events, not everyday.

Robes represent humility in fiction — not cosplay in public.

Want to feel more Jedi-like?

Embrace earth tones. Dress with intention. Let function be your form.

But real Jedi-ness is worn **in your conduct**, not your cloak.

✕ Jedi Do Not Believe Yoda Is Real

He's a symbol. A guide. A fiction with powerful truths.

But we live in this universe. We walk this world.

Worshiping fictional figures removes the responsibility of *embodying* the teachings.

✕ Jedi Do Not Worship George Lucas

Respect his work? Yes.

Admire his storytelling? Absolutely.

But worship? No.

He's a storyteller — not a prophet.

And like all stories, his work invites us to build something of our own.

✕ Jedi Do Not Let Emotions or Bias Cloud Judgment

We feel — deeply.

But we train so that **emotion informs us**, not controls us.

We use:

· **Meditation**
· **Self-awareness**

· **Reflection**

...to recognize when we're being pulled by bias or fear. Jedi don't suppress emotion — we learn to *respond*, not react.

✗ *Jedi Do Not Bully*

No posturing. No shouting.
    No "I'm right because I'm a Master" nonsense.
    A Jedi does not dominate — they guide.
    Even in disagreement, a Jedi remains composed, respectful, and ethical.

    Power without compassion is not strength — it's tyranny.

✗ *Jedi Do Not Infringe on Free Will*

You can offer knowledge.
    You can offer support.
    But you cannot force change.

    A Jedi is a light — not a leash.

There are exceptions, of course — when harm to others must be prevented.
    But even then, we tread carefully. Mindfully. With minimal force.

Process One Conclusion: Removing the Impurities

So what did we just do?
    We removed misconceptions. We burned off cultural residue.
    We cleared space for something honest, grounded, and functional.
    You're beginning to see the shape of the Jedi you'll become.
    But we can't define ourselves by what we reject. Now that we've cleared the

forge, it's time to begin building.

Before we move forward — you've got some training to do.

Jedi Homework: Forge Assignment One

This is a reflection-based assignment. There's no deadline. Take one week, take two. What matters is **depth over speed**.

1. Reconnect with Your Star Wars Inspiration

- Pick your favorite **Jedi media**:
- Film, Series, Comic, Novel, and/or Game.
- Watch, read, and/or play with intent.
- **Take notes** on how the Jedi act:
- What traits do they embody?
- What patterns do you see?
- What makes them Jedi in your eyes?

2. Trait Reflection

- After gathering your list of Jedi traits:
- Compare them to the **Five Traits of the Jedi** in the Jedi Circle:
- Patience
- Empathy
- Equity
- Accountability
- Decorum
- Compare them to the upcoming chapter: *What Jedi Are.*
- Journal:
- Where does your list match?

- Where does it differ?
- Why do you think that is?

3. Practice the Five Jedi Practices

Revisit the **Five Practices** of the Jedi:

- Meditation
- Physical Fitness
- Diplomacy
- Awareness
- Self-Discipline

Now try this:

- Assess which ones you already do daily.
- Brainstorm how to begin practicing the rest.
- Draft a **2-week Jedi Schedule** to begin integrating all five.

Workbook Section

Journal Prompts

- What traits stood out most in the Jedi you observed?
- Which misconceptions above challenged you?
- What does "being Jedi" mean to you — *right now*?

Daily Meditation Prompt

· Sit quietly and reflect:

"What do I need to let go of to walk this path clearly?"

Affirmation

"I am not here to pretend. I am here to practice."

Forging Process Two: Taking Shape

Now that we've addressed some misconceptions, let's focus on shaping what it means to live as a Jedi. This section begins the next stage of your training by introducing the core traits a Jedi strives to embody. These traits should be recognizable in our fictional inspiration and pass the **APBP Test**: Is it **Applicable**, **Practical**, **Beneficial**, and **Positive**?

To shape our path, we must ask:

What is a Jedi?

What do we represent?

How do we live it daily?

This section presents the values at the heart of Jedi living. Each one will be followed by journal prompts and actionable reflections to help you begin shaping your own Jedi path.

Jedi Are Patient

"Patience. Use the Force. Think." — Obi-Wan Kenobi

Patience isn't about sitting still—it's the *active practice* of being present with the process. It's trusting timing without forcing outcomes.

Sometimes patience is passive, like waiting in line. Sometimes it's active, like continuing to train while you wait for a door to open. Jedi patience means knowing when to move and when to breathe.

🧘♂Journal Prompt:

When was the last time patience helped you make a better decision?

When was the last time impatience led to regret?

Jedi Are Respectful

"The Jedi are guardians of peace and justice..." — Obi-Wan Kenobi

Respect is the everyday application of kindness and consideration. Jedi respect others' time, space, and boundaries—and also show respect inwardly.

Hold the door. Say thank you. Don't ghost people. Don't insult yourself. Respect begins in the small, daily choices.

🧘♀ Journal Prompt:

What's one respectful act you've done recently?

What's one area you could show more respect to *yourself*?

Jedi Are Disciplined

Discipline isn't about strictness—it's about *daily dedication*. It's showing up when it's hard, choosing your long-term goals over short-term comfort.

Discipline means following through. It's not perfection—it's consistency.

Journal Prompt:

Where in your life are you consistent?

Where do you struggle to follow through?

Jedi Are Calm

"Train yourself to let go of everything you fear to lose." — Yoda

Jedi feel deeply—but we don't let emotions control us. Calm isn't absence of feeling; it's *clarity through emotion.*

You can be angry and still act with compassion. You can be grieving and still hold space for others. Jedi calm is anchored presence.

Journal Prompt:

How do you personally return to calm?

What tools help you stay grounded under pressure?

Jedi Are Strong

Jedi strength is resilience—not domination. It's the strength to ask for help, to get back up, to keep going.

Sometimes strength is silent. Sometimes it's fierce. Always, it's rooted in purpose.

Journal Prompt:

What kind of strength shows up most in your life—emotional, mental, physical, spiritual?

What is one area you'd like to build strength in?

Jedi Are Reliable

Reliability means people know where they stand with you. It's not about saying *yes* to everything—it's about being *honest* and consistent.

"I can't right now" is reliable. So is "I'll be there" followed by *actually showing up.*

Journal Prompt:

How do others describe your reliability?

Where could you be more honest with your time and energy?

Jedi Are Objective

We all have biases. Jedi work to see beyond them—seeking clarity before reaction, listening before judgment.

Objectivity doesn't mean you lack opinion. It means you strive to *see the full picture* before drawing conclusions.

Journal Prompt:

When was the last time you changed your mind about something?

What helped you do it?

Jedi Are Observant

Awareness is one of our Five Practices for a reason. You can't respond wisely to what you don't see.

Observant Jedi notice their environment, others' needs, and their own inner states. They act *with* awareness—not on autopilot.

Journal Prompt:

Describe a time when noticing a small detail made a big difference.

What patterns do you tend to overlook?

Jedi Are Dedicated

"A Jedi's strength flows from the Force." — Yoda

Dedication is the quiet promise: *I choose this path again today.*

You will fail. You will fall short. You will question yourself. And you will get back up. Jedi choose this life not once—but every morning.

Journal Prompt:

What keeps you on this path?

What does Jedi dedication look like for you right now?

Workbook Assignment

Core Practices

Continue practicing your Five Fundamentals:

- **Meditation**
- **Physical Expression**
- **Diplomacy**
- **Awareness**
- **Self-Discipline**

The Nine Virtues – APBP Test

For each of the above nine traits:

- Reflect on whether the trait is **Applicable**, **Practical**, **Beneficial**, and **Positive** in your life.
- Rate yourself 1–10 on how strongly you embody that trait today.
- Choose one trait to work on more intentionally over the next week.

Jedi in Fiction

For each virtue, list one Jedi from canon, Legends, or fan-fiction who embodies it. What makes them an example of that trait?

This is not about perfection. This is about shape. You are the blade in the forge. And each reflection, each practice, helps you take form.

Forging Process Three: Slow Cooling

We've begun shaping ourselves through principles and clearing misconceptions. Now we slowly reinforce those changes — not through philosophy alone, but through consistent, grounded action. These are the daily applications of the Jedi Path.

Jedi Help Others

Helping others is a core Jedi trait — but not a command to burn yourself out. Jedi are not martyrs. Nor are they servants at the whim of anyone who demands help. Instead, Jedi support where and how they are able — with boundaries.

Helping can look like:

- Offering a kind word or calm presence.
- Supporting a friend during illness or hardship.
- Carrying groceries, helping someone move.
- Holding space, listening, or getting out of the way when appropriate.

Reflection Prompt:

When was the last time you helped someone without being asked? What did it require of you — emotionally, physically, or mentally?

APBP Test Prompt:

Think of your current go-to way of helping others.

- Is it Applicable to your life right now?
- Practical with your resources?
- Beneficial to you and the person?
- Positive for both your health and theirs?

Jedi Render Aid

Giving isn't only about money. Jedi give what they can — time, energy, blood, effort, kindness. You don't need wealth to be generous.

Aid can include:

- Donating blood or plasma.
- Giving food, blankets, or supplies.
- Volunteering with shelters, community orgs, or online projects.
- Mentoring or teaching.

Remember: Jedi are not the charity — they are a source of strength. You must be well to give well.

Awareness Check:

Are you over-extending yourself? Helping beyond your means?

Reflection Prompt:

What are you currently able to give? Be honest. What's one way you can give without draining your emotional or financial reserves?

Jedi Defend Those in Need

We've updated this phrase from "Defend the Weak" to "Defend Those in Need" — because language matters. No one is less-than for needing help.
Defense includes:

- Removing yourself (and others) from danger.
- Using your voice to stop escalation.
- Calling for help, being a good witness.
- Standing up for someone being bullied or mistreated.
- Learning martial arts or self-defense to empower confidence and protection.

"The best defense is not to be there." – Jedi Living Self-Defense Principle
Suggested Resource:
Verbal Judo by George J. Thompson – a foundational work on nonviolent de-escalation.
Scenario Reflection:
Recall a moment when you felt the urge to defend someone.
What stopped you?
What skills or support would have helped in that moment?
Ethical Balance Prompt:
How do you decide when to step in, and when to let someone face their challenge with your emotional support rather than direct involvement?

Forging Process Three: Slow Cooling (Part Two)

We now enter into the daily rituals and social behaviors that anchor the Jedi identity. These next two elements — meditation and diplomacy — serve as both inner and outer practices of peace.

Jedi Meditate

Surprised it took this long to get to meditation? Fair. But here we are — and meditation is a pillar of the Jedi lifestyle. It has been since the beginning, in fiction and in practice.

Meditation clearly passes the APBP Test:

✔ Applicable – countless cultures and traditions practice it

✔ Practical – neuroscience backs it for stress, memory, and focus

✔ Beneficial – it improves clarity and resilience

✔ Positive – it ripples outward through our interactions

There's no one way to meditate. What matters is intention and consistency. Let's look at a few ways to bring this into your life.

♂ Walking Meditation

Ideal for when you're active or restless. Walk slowly and attentively — in a park, around the block, or at the beach. Observe everything. Feel the wind. Hear the birds. Smell the earth. Let your awareness be full.

Practice Prompt:

Go for a 10-minute walk today and pay attention with all five senses.

What surprised you?

"I Don't Have Time" Meditation

You're at work. Or school. Life is chaotic. What can you do? Breathe deeply. Silently repeat a line from the Jedi Code that applies. It's a Jedi mantra in the moment.

"There is no chaos; there is harmony."

"There is no ignorance; there is knowledge."

Practice Prompt:

Choose a line from the Jedi Code that helps you the most right now.

Repeat it three times with full focus.

Star Meditation

Lie down, gaze at the stars (or close your eyes and imagine them). Focus on a single star. Picture its light growing brighter, then filling your body. Imagine carrying that star within you.

Reflection Prompt:

When do you feel most connected to the Force? Try this meditation on that night.

Final Tip:

Don't wait for the "right" conditions. Meditate daily, even for just 2 minutes. The habit matters more than the length.

Jedi Use Diplomacy

Diplomacy is often portrayed in fiction as Jedi Mind Tricks — quick manipulations for peaceful outcomes. But real Jedi don't override free will. We engage with empathy, knowledge, and presence.

True diplomacy begins with:

Knowing Your Audience

What do you know about this person? Their values, fears, patterns?

Can you anticipate their reaction and guide it toward calm?

Active Listening

Don't prepare a response. Listen to understand. Ask clarifying questions. Repeat back what you hear.

"What I'm hearing is..."
"Help me understand..."

This builds trust and allows people to feel heard — which often defuses conflict before it begins.

Gathering Information

Ask: What is their goal? What's yours? Is there common ground?

Build consensus through open dialogue, not dominance.

Practice Prompt:

In your next conversation, try asking three clarifying questions before offering your view.

Respect is the Bridge

Respect doesn't mean agreement — it means acknowledging the other's humanity. It sets the stage for openness.

"No one is entitled to a fight." – Jedi Cabur Sennar

You're not required to escalate, respond, or argue. Sometimes, silence or walking away is the most Jedi response available.

Reflection Prompt:

When did your calm presence prevent a situation from escalating?

What did you do — and how did others respond?

APBP Test Prompt:

Does your approach to conflict honor Jedi values? Is it Applicable in real life, Practical to use, Beneficial to both sides, and Positive in the long run?

Forging Process Three: Slow Cooling (Part Three)

We close out this process with one final cornerstone of the Jedi Way — not a dramatic lightsaber duel or great battle, but the quiet, subtle impact of guiding others.

Jedi Guide Others

Surprise! This isn't just about being a Jedi Master with a crew of Padawans trailing behind you. Guidance comes in many forms — and most of them are quieter than you'd expect.

Leading by Example

The simplest and most powerful form of guidance: just be a Jedi.

Live the path. Show patience, presence, discipline, and peace. You don't need to lecture or recruit.

You just need to live your values and let others notice.

Reflection Prompt:

Who has guided *you* in your life just by the way they live?

How can you do the same?

The Jedi Mentor

Eventually, someone may ask for your insight. They may want help, support, or a path to follow. If so, be a *mentor*, not a master.

Don't give them your answer sheet. Give them tools, questions, encouragement. Remind them that the Jedi Path is personal, not prescriptive.

> *"You're not building a clone of yourself. You're helping another person build their own path."*

Practice Prompt:

What's one lesson from your own journey you'd share with someone just starting out?

Guide, Don't Convert

Not everyone will want to become a Jedi — and that's okay. Your job is not to recruit. It's to be present when needed and offer support when asked.

The Jedi Way respects individual paths. Help others find harmony and peace, even if their answers look different from yours.

Reflection Prompt:

Can you support someone's growth, even if their philosophy differs from yours?

Process Three: Final Assignment

Let's bring it all together. You've studied the fiction. You've reflected on the traits. Now it's time to **take action**.

Wellness Goals – The Five Areas

Set *realistic*, *attainable*, and *Jedi-aligned* goals in each of these areas:

- **Physical Wellness**
- **Emotional Wellness**

- **Intellectual Wellness**
- **Spiritual Wellness**
- **Community Service**

Use the following example for inspiration:

- **Physical**: Cut out soda. Run 3 miles. Train for 5 press-ups (handstand push-ups).
- **Emotional**: Build a zazen habit. Heal from heartache.
- **Intellectual**: Learn ASL. Read 10 new books this year.
- **Spiritual**: Solidify beliefs about the Force and life after death.
- **Community**: Get 100 hours of service with a mentorship program.

Practice Integration

Now, create a basic *daily plan* to support those goals.

How will you practice Jediism consistently?

Example

- Set a 10-minute reminder for nightly zazen.
- Adjust workouts to support fitness goals.
- Study ASL for 15 minutes a day.
- Add spiritual books to your reading list.
- Dedicate one day a week to volunteer work.

The Goal: Sustainable Jedi Living

Start small. Focus on consistency, not perfection.

"One step at a time, Jedi. You have a whole life to refine the path."

Your lifestyle *is* your legacy. Every small daily practice builds your foundation. This isn't about long-term dreams (yet). This is about immediate wins. Create momentum. Build confidence. Let your actions ripple outward.

Journal Prompt:

What are your five wellness goals for this year?

What Jedi practices will you use to support them?

APBP Check:

Are these goals Applicable to your life, Practical in your current situation, Beneficial to your growth, and Positive for those around you?

Forging Process Four: Grinding

We've established our path by exploring our inspiration and applying Jedi principles through daily practices and clear goals. So far, we've heated the metal, hammered out a rough shape, and let it cool — shaping ourselves in the forge of Jedi living. Now comes the grinding: where we define the edges of our path with precision and experience.

This is where we get out into the world and *live* it. Where theory becomes application.

To do that, we begin with one of the Jedi's core tenets:

Jedi Seek Peace

The Sith Code (introduced in *Knights of the Old Republic*) famously begins:

"Peace is a lie."

A Sith I once knew believed that line wholeheartedly — that true peace was an illusion. And honestly? I get where he was coming from. If you define peace as an absence of all conflict, then yeah, it might seem unattainable.

But Jedi understand that peace is not a static ideal — it's a dynamic, multifaceted pursuit. It's not just about ending wars or silencing the noise. Peace can be found in moments, in mindset, in choices.

Peace of mind. Peace in the face of stress. Peace in how we interact with others. Peace as the end of internal struggle.

Let's focus on one of the most accessible kinds of peace: the resolution of *daily conflict.* Not the kind on battlefields, but the kind in your gut when the alarm goes off and your body screams "Snooze." Need versus want. Intention versus impulse.

The Four Steps to Jedi Emotional Clarity

Here's a Jedi process I recommend — a simple but powerful way to move through emotional conflict toward peace:

1. **Acknowledge**
2. **Explore**
3. **Accept**
4. **Act**

Let's break it down with a real-world Jedi lens.

Acknowledge

Call yourself out. *What am I feeling right now?*

Anger. Frustration. Joy. Fear. Conflict.

Even if you're not sure yet — give it a name. That conscious act puts you back in control. It gets the mind working and creates distance between you and your primal reaction.

"We cannot control how we feel. Only how we choose to handle our

feelings."
   — *Qui-Gon Jinn*

Identifying the emotion is the Jedi's first tool.

Explore

Ask: *Why am I feeling this?*
   Conflict? Okay, why?
   Because I don't want to go to work?
   Why not? I'm tired.
   Why am I tired? I stayed up late gaming.
   Ah. Self-inflicted. Time management fail.
   This process often reveals the *real* root — and lets you ask a better question: *What's the best response?*

Accept

This is the tough one.
   You've uncovered the truth — now *own* it.
   Don't argue with yourself. Don't inflate the drama. Just face it.
   You stayed up too late. You're not a bad Jedi — just a tired one. Acceptance turns frustration into understanding. And understanding leads to clarity.

Act

Put your realization into motion.
   This is the "lightsaber ignition" moment.
   No more philosophizing. Now you move.
   Maybe you get up and go to work anyway. Maybe you schedule better sleep. Maybe it's a deeper issue that takes time. But peace is not found by thinking. It's found in *doing*.
   The Jedi path doesn't end in reflection — it ends in action.

Example in Practice

> **Feeling**: *Happy*
>> **Why**: *A respected peer acknowledged my efforts.*
>> **Accept**: *That's hard for me to receive, but I trust their judgment.*
>> **Act**: *I'll keep growing — enjoy the moment without letting it make* me complacent.

Breathe. Smile. Peace.

Jedi Workbook: Peace Practice

Reflection Prompt:

Think of a recent moment where you experienced emotional friction or conflict (external or internal).

- What were you feeling?
- What was the root of that feeling?
- Did you accept the truth of it?
- What would "right action" have looked like in that moment?

Daily Exercise:

Practice the 4-step Jedi Peace Process today:

1. Acknowledge one emotion that arises strongly.
2. Explore it honestly — ask "why" until you hit the root.
3. Accept the truth, however inconvenient.
4. Act — even if the action is small.

Repeat tomorrow. And the next day. Until it becomes a habit.

APBP Test:

Does this practice pass the Jedi test?

- **Applicable** – Can I do this today? ✔
- **Practical** – Can I live by this in real life? ✔
- **Beneficial** – Does it improve my mindset and well-being? ✔
- **Positive** – Does it have a constructive impact on others? ✔

Looks like a Jedi win.

Jedi Seek and Encourage Knowledge

If there's one thing I've always loved about the Jedi Path, it's this:

> *Jedi* love *knowledge.*
> *And better yet — they encourage it in others.*

This isn't just about becoming a human encyclopedia. Jedi aren't trivia lords. Knowledge in the Jedi sense is dynamic, diverse, and deeply personal.

Each Jedi is pulled toward different interests. Some dive into meditation or philosophy, others explore diplomacy, galactic history, or physical sciences. I've met Jedi fascinated by environmentalism, martial arts, music theory, politics, languages, ancient cultures, neuroscience. You name it.

This diversity of interest means Jedi communities become natural hubs of shared insight. I've had some of my most educational conversations with Jedi from across the globe — learning how their governments work, how people live, and what values they hold close. That's the beauty of the information age: we're globally connected students in one great Jedi classroom.

Jedi Are Eternal Students

This book exists because of that mindset. Jedi live with what's often called **Beginner's Mind** — an approach that doesn't let the illusion of expertise block further learning. That mindset fuels everything.

Take Jedi Gatherings. You'll often find workshops on seemingly basic topics — say, meditation. I've meditated most of my life. I've read dozens of books, tried countless techniques. Still, I go to the workshop *bright-eyed and ready to learn.* Why?

Because a new viewpoint might shift everything. A personal story might click in a way theory never could. Or maybe I don't learn a new technique — but I pick up a *better way to teach* that technique.

If you're not open to the possibility of being surprised, you're stuck repeating only what you already know. Jedi make space for surprise. Jedi *learn forward.*

Knowledge is a Tool

Knowing how to change a tire? That's useful.

Knowing that Endor is a gas giant with nine moons and the "Forest Moon" is actually a satellite? Well... maybe not as helpful — unless you're crushing at Star Wars trivia night.

Still, to paraphrase Sherlock Holmes:

> *"All knowledge becomes useful to the detective."*

We never know what nugget will prove vital. But Jedi wisdom means staying open to learning — even on topics you *think* you've mastered.

This is the essence of science, too. Real knowledge is humble — it lets new data reshape the old.

Know What You Don't Know

There's wisdom in admitting ignorance.

I know nothing about running an auto repair shop. I'm barely functional in accounting. I couldn't explain cricket if my life depended on it. And that's okay.

Because saying "I don't know" unlocks something powerful: **curiosity**.

That's what Jedi lean into — not the pride of what they've mastered, but the excitement of what they've yet to discover.

The Teacher's Path

Eventually, knowledge ripens into something more:

Wisdom shared.

This is where Jedi become mentors — not just learners, but teachers. This can look like:

- Online forums
- Training programs
- 1-on-1 apprenticeships
- Or just grabbing coffee and saying, "Hey, here's a pitfall I learned the hard way..."

But with that comes responsibility. You don't become a mentor just because you feel smart one day. Jedi take time to live what they teach. They pass on knowledge **after** it's been tested in real life.

Think of it like this:

If you're wise and experienced now...
Imagine how much more you'll be in five years.

Let knowledge steep. Share it from overflow, not ego.

Knowledge Is a Platform, Not a Pedestal

This whole workbook exists because Jedi share what they learn. We write, we record, we teach, we pass on tools and truths — not to be worshipped, but to be surpassed.

> *We don't preserve wisdom so it stays frozen.*
> *We preserve it so the next Jedi can grow beyond it.*

The point isn't to venerate the old teachings. The point is to create a platform for the next generation to launch from. Build the base, then let them fly.
   That's how knowledge becomes legacy.

Jedi Reflection Practice

Journal Prompt:

- What's something you've recently realized you *don't know?*
- How did that realization make you feel — and what did it inspire?
- What kind of knowledge do you feel drawn toward learning next?

Daily Exercise:

- Ask one person (friend, coworker, fellow Jedi) about something *they* know that you don't. Let it spark a new rabbit hole.
- OR: Pick a random subject from a library, podcast, or YouTube deep dive. Learn one new thing today — no matter how trivial.

APBP Test:

Does seeking and sharing knowledge pass the Jedi standard?

- **Applicable** – Can I practice this daily? ✓
- **Practical** – Is this helpful to real-life growth? ✓
- **Beneficial** – Does this bring value to me and others? ✓
- **Positive** – Does this foster openness, learning, and humility? ✓

This is how Jedi live. Students. Teachers. Legacy builders.

Jedi Seek Serenity

Let's address the glow-elephant in the room:

Aren't peace and serenity the same thing?

In everyday language, sure. They're often used interchangeably. But within Jedi philosophy, there's a subtle (yet powerful) difference.

When we say "Jedi Seek Peace," we're usually talking about the *end of conflict.* Inner conflict. Outer conflict. Violence. Disruption.

But **Serenity** is something else.

Serenity is the *state* we return to.

It's not just the absence of conflict — it's the presence of calm.

It's balance in action. It's trust in the flow. It's confidence without control.

Passion and Serenity

When I first simplified the Jedi Code into practical phrases, I boiled this one down to:

"Find serenity through your passion."

The idea is simple: when you do what you love, serenity follows.

That feeling of being *in flow*. Focused. Fulfilled. Free.

Whether it's painting, lightsaber training, baking, designing apps, solving puzzles — when you fully engage in something that brings you alive, your mind and emotions align. That's serenity.

But it's not just about pleasure. It's about *meaningful* engagement. Purposeful energy. Bliss with direction.

Serenity is Balance

Conflict isn't always explosive. Sometimes it's quiet and internal —

like wanting to play all day when you've got work due.

This inner tug-of-war is often a sign of imbalance: between *what we want* and *what we need.* Between *our passions* and *our responsibilities.* Serenity doesn't come from avoiding one or the other — it comes from integrating both.

Here's the thing:

- Only doing what you *have* to do drains your spirit.
- Only doing what you *want* to do can wreck your future.

Serenity is found in the dance between the two.

Live your passion — and structure your life to support it sustainably.

That means making a plan. Budgeting time. Saying no to burnout.

Dreams matter. But dreams without structure are just fancy distractions.

Acceptance is Peace. Security is Serenity.

Two mantras. Both essential Jedi tools.

Acceptance is Peace – When we accept the people, events, and world around us for what they are (not what we wish they were), we stop resisting reality. That dissolves a huge source of tension.

Security is Serenity – When we feel safe in who we are and the path we've chosen, we move through life with calm confidence.

Serenity doesn't mean life will be easy. It doesn't mean nothing goes wrong.

It means that no matter *what* happens, we *know ourselves*. We know our principles. We know our capacity to adapt, endure, and act.

We flow with the current...

But we don't forget we have a paddle.

Jedi Reflection Practice

Journal Prompt:

- What does serenity feel like *for you?* When was the last time you truly experienced it?
- Where in your life are your *passions* and *responsibilities* currently out of balance?
- What steps could bring more structure to your dreams — without crushing their spirit?

Daily Exercise:

- Pick one thing you *love* to do that you haven't made time for lately. Do it for 10 minutes today — no guilt.
- Then pick one thing you've been *avoiding* that's essential to your responsibilities. Handle it today — with Jedi presence.
- Before bed, reflect: how did it feel to honor both sides of yourself?

APBP Test:

Does pursuing serenity pass the Jedi standard?

- **Applicable** – Can I aim for this daily? ✓
- **Practical** – Is it sustainable in a real-world lifestyle? ✓
- **Beneficial** – Does it improve my mood, focus, and relationships? ✓
- **Positive** – Does it increase clarity, balance, and presence? ✓

Serenity is not a distant reward.

It's a byproduct of right alignment.

Of living the Jedi Way — in your own rhythm, with your whole being.

Jedi Seek and Encourage Harmony

"What might seem chaotic might simply be a pattern we haven't recognized yet."

Chaos is often considered the opposite of harmony. But let's be real — the line between them is a matter of perspective. A flock of birds might look like a swirling mess until you realize they're moving in perfect sync. Jazz can sound wild until you notice each note has its place. Just because you don't understand the pattern doesn't mean there isn't one.

Understanding the order isn't *required* for the order to exist.

That's the Jedi perspective.

The Pattern Within the Chaos

During a roundtable discussion on our Jedi YouTube channel, a Jedi named L. Christopher Bird shared something profound. One of his apprentices described the line, *"There is no chaos; there is harmony"* by saying:

> *"A single note cannot harmonize with itself."*

Think about that. Harmony requires multiplicity. Connection. Timing.

You are not an island. The galaxy is not an island.

We are notes in a much larger song.

A car crash might feel like pure randomness — until you look at the sequence of events. Small choices, chance encounters, timing, weather. It doesn't make it *justified*. It doesn't make it *fair*. But it does make it part of a chain. A system. A web.

This Isn't About Blame

Let's be clear: this isn't about assigning fault.

The "blame game" is a void with no bottom. You point fingers, get angry, and still wake up the next day holding the same pain.

Blame doesn't build harmony. It fractures it.

The better question isn't "Who did this?"

It's: **"What now?"**

Harmony isn't about pretending bad things don't happen. It's about how we move through them — how we contribute to the healing, the restoring, the rebuilding.

Jedi Balance Is Harmony

So-called "Grey Jedi" didn't invent balance. It's been a Jedi principle from the start.

We balance:

- Mind, Body, Spirit
- Nature and Technology
- Passion and Responsibility
- Discipline and Indulgence
- Play and Work

Life has its highs and lows — and harmony is about flowing between them without losing your core. We're not trying to control the melody. We're learning how to *add our note* to the song.

As George Gershwin put it:

"Life is a lot like jazz — it's best when you improvise."

You Are Part of the Song

You don't need a time machine to bring harmony to your life.

You don't need perfect knowledge of how the song started. You just need to *listen*. And then *respond* with awareness and care.

Jazz musicians know when to solo and when to support. When to lead and when to fade into the rhythm. So too do Jedi learn when to speak and when to listen. When to fight the current and when to let go.

Qui-Gon Jinn didn't resist the flow of life — he adapted. Anakin tried to control everything — and shattered under the weight of it. Balance is not control. It's not rigidity. It's presence, patience, and participation in something greater than yourself.

Jedi Reflection Practice

Journal Prompt:

- What area of your life feels "chaotic" right now?
- Is there a pattern you might not be seeing?
- How can you shift from trying to control everything to harmonizing with

what is?

Daily Exercise:

- Identify a "discordant" moment in your day — a conflict, frustration, or miscommunication.
- Take five minutes to reflect on it without blame. What were the moving parts? What was *your* note in the pattern?
- Ask: how can I move through this in harmony, not resistance?

APBP Test:

Does seeking harmony pass the Jedi standard?

- **Applicable** – Can I bring this to daily life? ✔
- **Practical** – Is it sustainable even when life gets messy? ✔
- **Beneficial** – Does it support peace, understanding, and emotional clarity? ✔
- **Positive** – Does it lead to wiser, calmer action? ✔

Harmony isn't about perfection.
  It's about participation.
  You're not here to fix the song — just to play your part well.

Jedi Seek the Force

We're going to explore the Force in greater detail later in the book, especially when we dive into the spiritual side of Jediism. But for now, let's talk about one essential truth:

Jedi seek the Force.

That's not the same as defining it.

It's not about memorizing lore or quoting Master Yoda.

It's about *living the question.*

What *is* the Force — for you?

The Ineffable Mystery

Since the early 2000s, I've personally defined the Force as **ineffable**. That word — ineffable — means "beyond words." It acknowledges the impossibility of putting something so vast, so personal, into a tidy little box.

And that's exactly why the Jedi seek it. Not to conquer it. Not to define it once and for all.

But to *explore* it.

The Tools of the Seeker

We've already covered the core tools Jedi use to seek the Force:

- **Knowledge** – Exposure to new ideas and belief systems
- **Meditation** – Quieting the mind to feel what exists beyond words
- **Awareness** – Tuning in to your surroundings, your emotions, your experiences

When used together, these tools don't give you answers — they give you questions worth living.

Magic, Science, and the Force

As the film *Thor* puts it:

> *"Magic is just science we haven't figured out yet."*

Some Jedi feel the Force in nature — in wind, waves, or starlight. Others see it in gravity, energy fields, and quantum theory. Still others experience it through love, synchronicity, or intuition.

The path is open. You are allowed to explore. And you are *encouraged* to do so.

Build Your Personal Practice

Your job isn't to adopt someone else's belief — it's to cultivate your own.

Meditation helps with that.

Experience helps with that.

Even contradiction helps with that. Especially when you challenge your assumptions and ask:

- What *feels* true to me?
- What patterns do I notice?
- What belief or metaphor actually matches my experience?

The Force is not a doctrine.

It's a question echoing through your life, waiting for you to listen.

Jedi Reflection Practice

Journal Prompt:

- What have you believed about the Force up to this point?
- What beliefs, religions, or spiritual concepts have shaped your view?
- Where do you see or feel the Force in your everyday life?
- If the Force is ineffable — how do *you* best connect to it?

Daily Exercise:

- Spend 10 minutes in a quiet space. No music, no agenda.
- Focus on your breath, the sensations on your skin, the sounds around you.
- When the mind wanders, return to the question: *What is the Force, right now, in this moment?*
- Afterward, write a sentence or two capturing what you felt or noticed.

APBP Test:

Does seeking the Force align with Jedi values?

- **Applicable** – Yes. You can seek the Force anytime, anywhere. ✓
- **Practical** – Yes. Meditation, study, and awareness are sustainable. ✓
- **Beneficial** – Yes. This practice fosters humility, wonder, and meaning. ✓
- **Positive** – Yes. It encourages connection, curiosity, and presence. ✓

Final Note for This Section

You don't have to *figure it all out* right now.
   You don't have to name it, claim it, or explain it.
   You just have to seek.
   And in that seeking — you are already walking the Jedi path.

Jedi Seek and Encourage Honesty

Honesty Starts With the Self

One of the foundational pillars of any good relationship — romantic, professional, mentor-apprentice — is open and honest communication. The other two? **Trust** and **Respect**. You can't have one without the others.

But let's focus on the kind of honesty that matters most on the Jedi Path:

> ***Self-Honesty*** *— no loopholes, no addendums. It's the bedrock of personal growth.*

If you can't be honest with yourself — about where you're at, what your limitations are, and what your habits reveal — then no amount of Jedi philosophy will get you where you want to go. Self-delusion is just another mask for ignorance. Jedi training starts where you actually are, not where you pretend to be.

Shine Light Into the Corners

The dark side isn't some outside force waiting to tempt you.

It's the place inside you that you refuse to look at.

Jedi seek the light — and sometimes that light is uncomfortable. It means facing your ego. It means acknowledging your excuses. It means accepting that growth takes effort, time, and sometimes the cold clarity of truth.

But once you're honest with yourself, you become powerful — because you know exactly what you're working with.

"I'm Just Being Honest!"

Let's be clear: Jedi honesty is **not** a permission slip to be an asshole.

The phrase "I'm just being honest" is often used to excuse rudeness, judgment, or laziness in communication. Jedi practice **decency** alongside honesty. That means:

- You don't have to overshare.
- You don't have to tear people down.
- You **can** be blunt — but choose *when* and *how* with care.

If you consistently find people "can't handle your honesty," it may not be them. Jedi embrace **diplomacy**, **awareness**, and **conflict resolution** as part of the path.

A Jedi's Dilemma: Tactical Deception?

The Jedi Rules of Behavior (from *Power of the Jedi Sourcebook*) note:

> *"A Jedi can allow others to believe incorrectly, lead others to incorrect conclusions by playing on their suppositions, or stretch the truth if the situation demands it."*

Technically? That's canon-friendly. But in practice, most modern Jedi don't like it. They'd rather be upfront. Truth reduces confusion. Clarity builds trust. Gossip, lies, and manipulation have no place here — even if some fictional Jedi act otherwise.

Real Talk: My Delay

I'll be honest with you. This book was originally meant to be released in **January 2018**.

But life happened:

- A breakup from the girl I had loved for over 15 years.
- My dog dislocated both front legs.
- My dad's cancer worsened and he passed away.
- I needed a second job to survive financially.

At first, I told myself, *"I'll get back to it once life calms down."* But once it *did,*

I played video games instead of writing. Escapism. No excuses. Eventually it took someone asking — repeatedly — *"How's the book going?"* And every time I had to say "I haven't worked on it," I cringed.

She filled the role my dad once held. She gave me that honest kick I needed. (Thanks, Alexandria.) Sometimes we need people who will be honest with us. Sometimes *we* need to be the one to deliver that honesty to ourselves.

Jedi Reflection Practice

Journal Prompt:

- Where in your life are you not being fully honest with yourself?
- What habits or excuses are holding you back from the Jedi you want to be?
- Are you allowing yourself to grow — or just giving yourself comfort?

Bonus:

- Who in your life can be honest with you in a constructive way?
- Who can you offer that same gift to?

Daily Practice:

The Mirror Check-In

- At the end of each day, take 2–5 minutes to reflect:
- Did I live today in line with my Jedi goals?
- Where did I fall short — and why?
- What is one small thing I can adjust tomorrow?

Do this consistently. Make it your final act before bed. The reflection habit alone will transform your path.

APBP Test:

Is honesty a Jedi practice?

- **Applicable** – Yes. It begins with self-reflection and applies to all relationships. ✓
- **Practical** – Yes. Honesty leads to clarity, integrity, and better communication. ✓
- **Beneficial** – Yes. Even painful truths lead to growth and wisdom. ✓
- **Positive** – Yes. When rooted in respect and diplomacy, honesty builds stronger bonds. ✓

Final Assignment:

Your Jedi Daily Grind

Jedi life is not fireworks. It's repetition.

It's the **grind** — the things you do every day without fanfare.

Here's an example schedule I once kept while working as a personal driver:

```
5:00 – 5:20 AM: Wake-up, Morning Routine
5:20 – 9:00 AM: Work
9:00 – 11:00 AM: Jedi Media (Socials, Journaling)
11:00 – 12:30 PM: Workout, Dog Walk, Lunch
12:30 – 3:00 PM: Projects, Career Search, Chores
3:00 – 4:00 PM: Meditation
4:00 – 8:30 PM: Work
8:30 – 10:00 PM: Dinner, Evening Routine, Jedi Reflection
10:00 PM – 5:00 AM: Sleep
```

It wasn't perfect. It was adaptable. But it gave structure.

Your assignment is to draft a rough daily schedule for your Jedi life.

Then live it.

Each night, do your mirror check-in.

After two weeks, write a journal entry about what you've learned:

- What worked?
- What didn't?
- What surprised you?
- What changed?

Jedi life begins where excuses end.

Forging Process Five: Hardening

Jedi Honor Personal Pursuits

From Shaping to Strengthening

We've spent the last four processes shaping your foundation — now we begin the **hardening** phase. This is where we test what's been forged. We apply pressure, heat, and challenge to solidify what it means to *live* as a Jedi in the world.

In this section, we focus on what **Jedi Honor** — the values we carry into real life, the personal pursuits that flavor our journey, and how we apply Jedi ideals beyond the Temple walls.

You've got the theory. You've walked the practice. Now it's time to test it in the fire of real life.

The Jedi Path & Your Path Are Not Always the Same

Let's talk hobbies.

Jedi love hobbies. Some of us do martial arts. Some run obstacle races. Some are obsessed with Go, or build lightsabers, or volunteer in the ER. These pursuits often *align* with Jedi principles — but they are not, by themselves, what *make* you a Jedi.

Just because something feels Jedi-like doesn't mean it is *the Jedi Path.*

You don't get extra Jedi points because you've been in law enforcement.
Or mastered Reiki.
Or have twenty years of fencing under your belt.
That's your story — not your *status*.

Jediism Is Not Cosplay for Your Résumé

People sometimes say:

"I've done [insert skill here] for 10 years. That should make me a Jedi Knight, right?"

Nope.

Because Jedi Knight is not a merit badge. It's not an award for time served. It's a reflection of who you are in daily life — right now — and how you live the Jedi Way.

Jediism supports your personal pursuits. But it does not *require* them. You can be a Jedi and never step foot in a dojo. You can be a Jedi and hate running. You can be a Jedi who knits scarves and studies marine biology. As long as you live by the Path, it counts. Your life *is* the practice ground.

My Example: Mud Runs & Jedi Fog

I love running Spartan Races and obstacle courses. They bring me that *Luke on Dagobah* kind of clarity. The struggle. The sweat. The solitude. For me, they *connect* to the Jedi Path.

But do they *make* me a Jedi?

No.

I could run 50 races and still fail to live by Jedi values. And another Jedi could run one and say, "Nope. Never again." Neither of us is more or less Jedi because of it. These pursuits may **support** our journey, but they are not *the journey.*

Jedi Circle Alignment

- **Virtue**: *Self-Honesty* — Knowing what supports your growth vs. what strokes your ego
- **Trait**: *Decorum* — Not demanding titles or recognition for unrelated achievements
- **Goal**: *Proficiency* — Using your interests to strengthen Jedi living, not define it

Journal Reflection

Take 10 minutes to explore the following:

- What hobbies or personal pursuits currently support your Jedi journey?
- Are there any you've used to justify "status" or shortcuts on the path?
- What do you do because it helps you grow vs. because it looks good on paper?

Daily Practice:

Audit Your Path vs. Your Pursuits

Choose one activity you engage in weekly (martial arts, gaming, meditation, writing, etc.) and ask:

- Why do I do this?
- What part of the Jedi Path does it connect to?
- Does it help me become a better Jedi — or just feel like one?

Write down your answers. Be honest. Then keep what works. Let go of what doesn't.

APBP Test:

Do personal pursuits support Jediism?

- **Applicable** – Yes, if integrated mindfully into your Jedi life ✓
- **Practical** – Yes, as long as they aren't mistaken for "requirements" ✓
- **Beneficial** – Yes, if they contribute to your growth, insight, or discipline ✓
- **Positive** – Yes, when they inspire others or reinforce your personal practice ✓

Jedi Reminder:

"Love what you do. Embrace your additions. Just remember — there's a difference between your path and the Path."

When in doubt, breathe. Then *be a Jedi.*

Jedi Honor Personal Paths

This section continues the thread from before — only now we step into deeper waters: faith, worldview, and belief.

A common question:

"Is Jediism a religion?"

Answer:

Yes. And also... not always.

Jediism can function like a religion, especially when it gives someone meaning, purpose, and spiritual practice. But it's also a **philosophy** — a path people walk from many different origins. You'll find Jedi who are:

- Christian
- Buddhist
- Atheist
- Pagan
- Taoist
- Sikh
- Jedi-only

And that diversity is okay. More than okay — it's expected.

Spiritual wellness is a **core** Jedi principle. But the specifics? That's personal. Jediism does not demand you believe in "the Force" in one specific way. What matters is how your beliefs help you live by the Jedi Path.

Jedi Faith ≠ Jedi Status

Let's be clear:

"I've been a Buddhist monk for 20 years."
"I studied under a Sufi mystic."

"I've been doing meditation since the womb."

That's cool. That's impressive. But it doesn't earn you Jedi titles. Your beliefs may *complement* Jediism. They may *enrich* your Jedi journey. But they are not a substitute for living as a Jedi.

As Jedi, we **honor individuality**.

We **honor the many faces of the Force**.

And we **do not gatekeep enlightenment**.

Jedi Circle Alignment

- **Virtue**: *Gratitude* — Appreciate your spiritual tools, without arrogance
- **Tenet**: *The Force* — Embrace it as personal, present, and ineffable
- **Goal**: *Discover* — Let your beliefs deepen your connection to the Jedi Path

Journal Reflection:

- What spiritual or philosophical ideas do you currently follow?
- How do they align with Jedi values?
- Where do they diverge? Can they coexist peacefully?

Daily Practice:

Integrative Reflection

In your next meditation, reflect not on "what you believe," but rather:

- What do my beliefs help me *do*?
- How do they shape my behavior and compassion?
- How do they connect to the concept of the Force?

Jedi Honor Society's Laws

Now we wade into more complex terrain: Jedi vs. the real world.
At first glance, this one rubs people the wrong way:

"Honor society's laws? What if they're unjust?"

A fair question. But like most Jedi teachings, this one is layered.
Let's break it down.

Example One (Fictional):

Qui-Gon Jinn on Tatooine

In *The Phantom Menace*, Qui-Gon says:

"I didn't come here to free slaves."

Tatooine is under Hutt control. The Jedi represent the Galactic Republic. Freeing slaves there would be viewed as an **act of war**. Instead, Qui-Gon navigates the system to free Anakin — working within the legal framework, even though he *despised* the system.
That's not weakness. That's **wisdom under fire**.

Example Two (Real Life):

Sometimes our countries enact unjust laws.
Sometimes voices are silenced. Rights are removed. History is whitewashed.

What do Jedi do then?

We fight. Not with lightsabers. But with votes, education, organizing, and strategic resistance. Change takes time, energy, and long-term commitment.
But Jedi *don't abandon the Path when it gets hard.* That's when we *double*

down.

When Systems Fail

Let's be honest: Some places are broken.

Some governments are corrupt, and some Jedi will find themselves in unsafe, unstable systems. This is where the *Jedi Method* becomes essential (we'll revisit this later).

As Qui-Gon said:

"I shall do what I must."

But that's not a license to go rogue. It's a reminder that Jedi must use judgment, courage, and wisdom — not ego.

Jedi Circle Alignment

- **Tenet**: *Peace* — The path of change without violence
- **Trait**: *Accountability* — Understanding when and how to act
- **Virtue**: *Self-Honesty* — Knowing your limits, strengths, and motivations
- **Goal**: *Service* — Work for justice *within* the system when possible

APBP Test:

Do Jedi honor society's laws?

- **Applicable** – Yes, this can be integrated into daily Jedi conduct ✓
- **Practical** – Yes, especially in democratic systems or advocacy channels ✓
- **Beneficial** – Yes, in promoting stability, safety, and ethical engagement ✓
- **Positive** – Yes, if used to promote long-term societal good ✓

Journal Reflection:

- Have you ever disagreed with a law or policy where you live?
- How did you respond — and what would a Jedi approach look like?
- Are there causes you can support that align with Jedi values?

Daily Practice:

Civic Jediism

Choose one issue you care about in your community or country.
Then do one of the following:

- Research a nonprofit or Jedi-aligned org working on it
- Register or confirm your voter registration
- Write a letter to a representative
- Share an educational post, respectfully and constructively

Small actions matter. Ripples grow.

Jedi Honor Their Students

A Jedi teaches. A Jedi guides.

But a Jedi also **listens**.

Too often, we forget that our students are not blank slates — they are individuals on their own journey. Some are young in age, others are simply new to the Jedi Path. And some may be older than you, but still at the beginning of *this* particular road.

To teach is to respect.
To respect is to listen.
To listen is to grow — together.

The Fresh Eye Principle

New perspectives matter. You may have heard the same question a thousand times — but to the student asking, it's brand new. Treat it with care. Engage with it. Let your patience become your strength. There's an old Jedi community lesson:

"Asked a Million Times."

It's about questions that come up over and over again — like Jedi temples, unity, or rewriting the Code. The real Jedi answer?

"Yes, I've heard this before — and I'm glad you're asking it now."

Jedi Are Not Clones

Students are not minions. They're not trophies. And they're not here to prop up your ego.

- Don't promote someone because you're lazy.
- Don't demand your students act like copies of yourself.
- Don't use students to validate your own identity.

Jedi honor their students by offering guidance — not control.

Jedi Circle Alignment

- **Trait**: *Empathy* — Respect the stage each student is in
- **Virtue**: *Guidance* — Lead without domination
- **Goal**: *Create* — Help foster new Jedi leaders

Journal Reflection:

- Think about someone you've helped or taught — formally or informally.
- Did you listen as much as you spoke?
- How can you improve your ability to nurture growth without controlling it?

Daily Practice:

Ask First. Teach Second.

Today, instead of correcting someone outright, try this:

1. Ask them how *they* see the problem.
2. Offer perspective, not a command.
3. Thank them for sharing their view.

Honor the process of learning by *trusting the learner.*

Jedi Honor Their Teachers

Not everyone finds their Yoda. Some of us find... three Jar Jars and a Darth Sidious before we meet a Qui-Gon. Still — Jedi honor the effort.

Even the worst "mentor" may teach us something valuable — even if it's just what *not* to do. Growth often comes not from a singular Master, but from a community. And sometimes, from a whole lot of trial and error.

> *"I never found my Jedi Master. But I found hundreds of Jedi voices —*
> *and each one taught me something."*

The Hidden Curriculum

You didn't get here alone.

- Maybe it was a teacher in school.
- Maybe a martial arts instructor.
- Maybe the author of a book you're reading right now (hint hint).

The fact remains: Someone gave their **time**, **energy**, and **resources** so you could grow. Honor that.

How to Honor a Teacher

It's not about blind loyalty. It's about *engagement.*

- Ask thoughtful questions
- Participate fully in the lesson
- Reflect and apply what's been shared
- Be present — be *with* them on the path

Bonus points if you laugh at their terrible jokes. (This is a test.)

Jedi Circle Alignment

- **Virtue**: *Erudition* — Value wisdom passed from others
- **Trait**: *Decorum* — Show respect through effort, not flattery
- **Goal**: *Discover* — Let lessons reveal new paths

Journal Reflection:

- Who has played the role of "teacher" in your life — Jedi or otherwise?
- What did they give you that stayed with you?
- Have you ever honored that gift with action, gratitude, or growth?

Daily Practice:

Mentor Memory

Reach out to one person who helped you learn something valuable.

Doesn't matter if it was recent or years ago.

Send a message. Write a letter. Leave a comment.

Just say:

"Thank you. You made a difference."

Jedi Honor the Organization(s)

Honoring doesn't mean worshipping.

It doesn't mean silence.

It doesn't mean pretending everything's okay.

To truly honor the organizations that helped us grow, we must hold them accountable. Respect is not blind allegiance — it is courageous integrity.

"To honor something is to challenge it to be better — not because you hate it, but because you love what it could be."

We Are Not the Pinnacle

The first mistake of Jedi organizations — both in fiction and reality — is acting like the goal is *now*. That *we* are the Jedi ideal.

Wrong. We are not the end. We are the foundation.

We build so others can build higher.

Honor your org not by defending its flaws, but by helping improve them. The

Jedi community is still young — and it needs strong, clear voices to help it mature.

Truth Will Ruffle Feathers

When you point out failures in leadership or structural mistakes, it will sting egos. You may be called a traitor, a hypocrite, or worse.

That doesn't mean you're wrong.

- Jedi honor the effort of those who built the community.
- Jedi acknowledge the time, money, and energy that went into it.
- But Jedi also speak up when things fall short of our ideals.

Silence is not respect.
Honesty is not betrayal.
Growth is the real *honor.*

Jedi Circle Alignment

- **Virtue**: *Self-Honesty* — See clearly, speak truth
- **Trait**: *Accountability* — Hold the path to its own standards
- **Goal**: *Proficiency* — Strengthen the structure for future Jedi

Journal Reflection:

- Think about a time you challenged something you were part of — a job, a relationship, a group.
- Was your criticism rooted in love or ego?
- How can you offer feedback in ways that encourage growth rather than division?

Daily Practice:

Constructive Honor

Look at a Jedi organization (online, offline, past, present) that has shaped your path.

- Identify **one thing they did well**.
- Identify **one area that could improve**.
- Write a respectful post, comment, or private message offering both appreciation and insight.

Jedi Honor the Path

This is it. The final Jedi Precept. The core beneath every concept we've explored so far.

You honor the Jedi Path not by quoting it. Not by talking about it. Not by debating canon or winning internet arguments.

*You honor the Path by **living** it.*

That means showing up — when it's hard. It means sticking to your ethics — when it's inconvenient. It means making the Jedi Way more than a label or hobby. It means choosing to be Jedi, even when no one is watching.

No One's Coming to Save You

There is no Jedi Police. There is no rank to fall back on. There is no Master watching your every move. You are your own Jedi. You are your own standard bearer. You are your own legacy.

Jedi Circle Alignment

- **Tenet**: *The Force* — The unifying ideal that underpins the path
- **Virtue**: *Commitment* — Stay the course
- **Goal**: *Service* — Let your actions reflect the teachings

Journal Reflection:

- Are you living the Jedi Path — or just reading about it?
- Where are your actions aligned with your values?
- Where do you still struggle — and what's one step you can take today to move closer to the Jedi you want to be?

Daily Practice:

The Jedi Mirror

Look at how you behaved over the last 24 hours.
Ask:

- Was I patient?
- Was I honest?
- Did I serve someone other than myself?
- Did I uphold peace, or stir conflict?

No judgment. Just awareness.
Honor the Path by continuing to walk it.

Conclusion: The Burnout Cycle

The Four-Week Jedi Challenge

Time to stress-test your discipline and your balance. This is an experimental overload. It's not about "winning." It's about *learning where your limits are* — and more importantly, how to return to balance when you go too far.

This is your Jedi version of trial by fire... with a cold plunge in between.

You'll follow a **four-week cycle**:

*Week One: **Overload***
*Week Two: **Cooldown***
*Week Three: **Reintegration***
*Week Four: **Overload++***

The goal isn't perfection — the goal is awareness.

Week One – Double-Time

Take your current Jedi routine... and double it.

- Meditation: Double the minutes
- Physical Fitness: Double the duration
- Study: Twice as much reading or lecture material
- Mindfulness: Add an additional practice or daily check-in

This is going to suck. Good.

You'll learn:

- Where your real limits are
- What parts of your practice feel forced vs. energizing
- Why *smart* programs have pacing and recovery built in

Caution: Don't hurt yourself. No one earns Jedi Points for injuries or burnout. If your body, mind, or spirit says "enough," listen.

Week Two – Cold Turkey

Let go. All of it.
You are not a Jedi this week.

· No meditation
· No physical workouts
· No Jedi study or philosophy
· No engaging with Jedi communities

This is *not* permission to be cruel, reckless, or self-destructive.

This is an intentional break.

Why? Because **attachment to the identity** can become a problem too. Let go, see how you feel, and notice what parts you miss — or don't.

Week Three – Resync

*Return to your **normal Jedi routine**.*

Reintroduce your daily Jedi habits and practices. The aim isn't to jump back into perfection. It's about finding rhythm again.

You'll notice:

· What routines return easily
· What feels resistant
· How your body/mind/spirit responds to regular training again

This week teaches you about **sustainability.**

Week Four – Jedi Overload+

*Not just double — **drench** yourself in Jedi.*

- Double your regular practices again
- Add new Jedi lessons: visit archives, read old articles, explore new lectures
- Revisit unfinished training modules or dive into new ones
- Journal or post about your experience
- Practice Jedi presence *everywhere* — work, home, public

Become the Force for a week. Total immersion.

Then...

Let it all go.

Return to normal. Reflect. And adjust.

Weekly Reflection Prompts

At the end of **each week**, answer the following:

1. **What was my energy level at the start of the week?**
2. **What changed during the week?**
3. **What surprised me about the process?**
4. **What insights did I gain about myself and the Jedi Path?**
5. **Did this week impact my relationships, work, or emotions?**
6. **What will I keep, change, or remove from my practice moving forward?**

Jedi Circle Alignment

- **Practice**: *Self-Discipline*
- **Virtue**: *Commitment*
- **Goal**: *Create* — A balanced, personalized Jedi routine

Final Thoughts from the Forge

This month is going to give you something most books never can:

Lived Experience.

Now you'll understand why we advocate balance. Why we warn against overexertion. Why moderation is baked into the Jedi Circle. You'll have gone through the fire — and through the silence. And you'll come out better for it.

No path is walked without hardship.

But you don't have to stumble blindly.

Let's move on to **Forging Process Six – Tempering** when you're ready. The path continues.

Forging Process Six: Tempering

Slow Down, Settle In

Overview: The Cooling Phase of the Forge

We've hammered out the ideals. We've faced the fire. We've ground the edges. Now we *temper* the blade.

This process isn't about pushing harder. It's about **letting the teachings settle**. It's a return to *simplicity*, to *structure*, and to *stability*. This phase reminds us: Jedi isn't just a title — it's a rhythm.

Your task is to slowly read through the **Additional Lectures** in this workbook. But *don't rush*. Highlight passages that resonate or conflict with you. Take time to weigh the ideas. Consider their truth against your own path. Reflect deeply.

While doing so, you'll be completing **three daily check-ins** for at least two weeks:

1. The Jedi Precepts Checklist
2. The Jedi Circle Inventory
3. The Rooney Mirror Test

The purpose? To build a quiet but powerful discipline — a rhythm of daily review and recalibration.

1. The Jedi Precepts Checklist

Each day, check off the qualities and behaviors you practiced. Add notes if anything stood out.

```
☐
Did Not Bully Others☐
Patient☐
Respectful and Courteous☐
Disciplined☐
```

```
Calm☐
Strong☐
Reliable☐
Objective☐
Observant☐
Dedicated☐
Helped Others☐
Defended Those in Need☐
Meditation☐
Used Diplomacy☐
Guided Others☐
Sought Peace☐
Sought and Encouraged Knowledge☐
Sought Serenity☐
Sought Harmony☐
Sought the Force☐
Sought Honesty☐
Personal Pursuits☐
Honored Students☐
Honored Teachers / Elders☐
Honored Society's Laws☐
Honored the Path
```

Reflection Journal Suggestion:

What stood out to you today? Did you fall short in any area? Where did you thrive?

2. The Jedi Circle Inventory

Use the **Jedi Circle** as a second self-check. How well did you align with these principles today?

The Five Practices

- **Diplomacy** – Resolved conflict or prevented one
- **Physical Fitness** – Moved your body in a healthy way
- **Self-Discipline** – Followed through on something

- **Awareness** – Practiced mindful presence
- **Meditation** – Took time to quiet your mind

The Five Tenets

- **Peace** – Chose calm over conflict
- **Knowledge** – Sought out learning
- **Serenity** – Kept a balanced heart
- **Harmony** – Worked with others or the moment
- **The Force** – Felt or followed your deeper purpose

The Five Traits

- **Equity** – Treated people fairly
- **Accountability** – Owned your actions
- **Patience** – Allowed things to unfold
- **Decorum** – Chose appropriate behavior
- **Empathy** – Sought to understand others

The Five Virtues

- **Gratitude** – Found something to be thankful for
- **Self-Honesty** – Reflected truthfully on your day
- **Erudition** – Learned or taught something
- **Guidance** – Offered wisdom to someone else
- **Commitment** – Stuck with the path despite obstacles

The Five Goals

- **Service** – Helped others help themselves
- **Defense** – Protected someone or something vulnerable
- **Proficiency** – Improved a Jedi-related skill
- **Create** – Built, designed, or shared something meaningful

- **Discover** – Moved toward purpose or meaning

3. The Rooney Mirror Test

Each evening, look into your eyes in the mirror and ask:

1. *Did I exercise and develop my body today?*
2. *Did I eat well today?*
3. *Did I learn something new today?*
4. *Did I make someone feel better today?*
5. *Did I take a positive step toward a major goal today?*

This external framework keeps you connected not just to Jedi ideals, but to *human flourishing.*

Assignment Instructions

Duration: Minimum 14 days
  Activity: Daily use of all three checklists
  Optional: Use a highlighter while reading Additional Lectures

Reflection Prompts (Use Weekly or Bi-Weekly)

- Which checklist item(s) were hardest to fulfill this week? Why?
- What surprised you about your Jedi consistency?
- Are you noticing changes in how you see the world?
- What old habits or beliefs are being challenged?
- What part of the Jedi Circle feels most natural to you? Most foreign?

Jedi Circle Alignment

- **Practice**: *Awareness*
- **Tenet**: *Harmony*
- **Virtue**: *Self-Honesty*
- **Goal**: *Discover* — how your Jedi life unfolds one quiet step at a time

Final Words of the Tempered Blade

This chapter isn't flashy.

But neither is peace.

And peace — true Jedi peace — takes repetition, habit, reflection, and forgiveness. This is where you learn to live it, one day at a time.

When you're ready, we'll move into **Forging Process Seven – Polishing**, where we begin refining what has now been formed.

Let the path settle into you.

Let it become natural.

Let it be yours.

Forging Process Seven – Completion

The Journey Begins Anew

Overview: Not the End, But the Turning Point

Jedi training doesn't end.

You've made it through the forge — shaped, cooled, and tempered. But what we've built here is **only the hilt of your lightsaber**, not the crystal that will power it. This book was never a "Five Steps to Jedi Mastery." It's a **map to the gate**, not the journey beyond it.

This chapter marks your *first step* — with clarity, tools, and values — into the larger world of Jedi philosophy and community. And with that comes your final assignment: *personal integration*.

The Assignment: Build Your Jedi Life

Take time with the following questions. They're not just journal prompts — they're the **seed of your individual Jedi path**. Answer them now, then revisit them **in one year**. See how you've changed, what's remained, and how the path has grown with you.

You are welcome to adapt, expand, or build your own version from these foundations.

Meditation & Inner Stillness

1. *What is your preferred meditation style, technique, or schedule?*
2. *How would you help another find their meditation rhythm?*

Physical Training & Discipline

1. *What does your fitness routine look like?*
2. *How would you help someone discover a fitness approach that works for them?*

Service & Creation

1. *What are you creating? (Projects, writing, art, systems, rituals?)*
2. *How do you fulfill the Jedi goal of Service?*
3. *How would you help another person find fulfillment through service?*

Values & Direction

1. *What do you view as essential to being a Jedi?*
2. (Consider: Jedi Traits, What Jedi Do, Seek, Honor, Avoid — in your own words.)

Spirituality & Belief

1. *What is your spiritual outlook or practice?*
2. (Force-focused? Naturalistic? Taoist? Agnostic? Mystical? Something else?)
3. *How would you help another person find their own spiritual perspective?*

The Path Ahead

1. *What does your Jedi training program look like now?*
2. (Do you study online? With a group? Use this book? Follow a self-guided path?)

Optional: Revisit After 1 Year

Schedule a return to this page in 12 months. Mark the date.

One Year Revisit Date: ____

Re-read your answers. Add new ones. See what's changed. Honor the evolving journey.

Final Thoughts

You've built a foundation of practice. You've embraced the wisdom of discipline, service, and awareness. Now, your path is yours to walk.As always:

> **Be a Jedi. In all ways. For all days.**
> —*Opie Macleod*

Jedi Circle Alignment

- **Practice**: *Self-Discipline*
- **Tenet**: *The Force*
- **Trait**: *Accountability*
- **Virtue**: *Commitment*
- **Goal**: *Proficiency*

Final Meditation Prompt

> "What does your Jedi life look like today — and what could it become tomorrow?"

Sit with it. Let it echo. And then — begin again.
Onward, Jedi.

4

Addition Lectures

The Jedi Method

Overview: Ethics for Everyday Jedi

Ethical decision-making is one of the least discussed yet most vital parts of
the Jedi Path. It often falls into the "goes without saying" category — but
what *does* a Jedi do when faced with difficult choices?

There's no single answer. No cheat code. No flowchart that neatly sorts out
life's messy complexity. Jedi philosophy doesn't pretend every situation has
a clean solution. But it *does* offer a method — a way to think, reflect, and act
with integrity across any situation.

Enter: **The Jedi Method.**

Why We Need a Method

I've stumbled. Hard. More than once.

Despite creating the Jedi Circle, and holding the path close to my heart, I
found myself without a *reliable internal check* for my decisions. I needed a way
to hold myself accountable — not just after the fact, but *before* choices were
made.

From that reflection, I created a simple framework:

Jedi Intent + Jedi Action = Jedi Outcome

It's not just catchy. It's how I train myself to live Jedi values *when it actually counts* — in real-life decisions, not in theory.

Let's Break It Down

1. Jedi Intent

This is your *why.*

Your purpose. Your motivation. Your intention going into an action.

Jedi Intent is guided by our Virtues, Tenets, and Goals*:*
Peace, Serenity, Harmony. Service, Guidance, Protection.
It's rooted in what Jedi seek — *as covered in Sections Four and Five.*

Examples:

- Helping someone because you care.
- Taking time for self-care because your wellness matters.
- Standing up for justice even when it's hard.

2. Jedi Action

This is your *how.*

How you behave. How you speak. How you engage with others — especially when challenged.

Jedi Action draws from What Jedi Do — *Section Three.*
This includes Patience, Awareness, Empathy, Diplomacy, and Service.

It's not enough to have good intentions — the *manner* in which you act matters.

Reflection:

- Did you stay calm?
- Did you practice compassion and self-discipline?
- Did you align with Jedi values *in action*, not just thought?

3. Jedi Outcome

This is your *what happened.*

The results. The consequences. The impact.

Here's the reality check:

You can do everything right — and things might still go wrong. That's life.

But if your Intent and Action aligned with Jedi values, you still stood in integrity.

Outcome matters, but it isn't everything. It's a teacher, not a judge.

"You can't predict how people will act, but you can control how you'll respond."
— Mass Effect

Ethics Breakdown

Ethical Lens: **Utilitarianism**

Description: The result matters most (greatest good).

Jedi Relevance: Jedi care about impact — but not at the cost of integrity.

Ethical Lens: **Intent Ethics**

Description: If your intentions were good, you did right.

Jedi Relevance: Jedi hold intention as one factor — not the only one.

Ethical Lens: **Deontological Ethics**

Description: Focus on duty and principle.

Jedi Relevance: Jedi action includes duty: justice, empathy, non-harm.

Jedi Ethics combines all three:

Intention (Why) + *Action* (How) = ⚭ *Outcome* (Result)

All are held in balance. None outweigh the others.

The Jedi Method Formula

Jedi Intent

Rooted in Jedi Virtues and Goals

(Sections 4 & 5)

Jedi Action

Reflected in Jedi Practices and Traits

(Section 3)

Jedi Outcome

Aligned with Jedi Tenets and Values

(Section 2 & 6)

Reflection Activity: Jedi Ethics in Real Life

Scenario Practice:

Pick a real-life decision (past or upcoming).

Walk it through the Jedi Method:

1. **What was/is your intent?**
2. **What actions did you take (or plan to take)?**

3. **What was the outcome or potential consequence?**
4. **Did your action reflect Jedi principles (honestly)?**
5. **Did it pass the APBP Test?**
6. ✔ Applicable
7. ✔ Practical
8. ✔ Beneficial
9. ✔ Positive

Write a short journal entry after each use.

Meditation Prompt:

"Am I acting as the Jedi I hope to be — in both purpose and presence?"

Sit with that. Breathe through it. Let it guide your response.

Jedi Circle Alignment

- **Practice**: *Awareness*
- **Tenet**: *Knowledge*
- **Trait**: *Accountability*
- **Virtue**: *Self-Honesty*
- **Goal**: *Service*

Final Notes

The Jedi Method is a lifelong tool.
Let it evolve as you grow.
Use it when you fall. Use it when you rise.
Use it when you're not sure what to do next.
Intent + Action = Outcome.
And no matter the outcome — *stay Jedi.*

Robes, Lightsabers, and Temples – Oh My!

The Myth vs. The Path

One of the biggest misconceptions new Jedi often bring with them is that Jediism is *about* robes, temples, and lightsabers. These iconic symbols are central to the **fictional** Jedi — and it's no wonder they spark the imagination. But the Jedi path in real life? It's much deeper, simpler, and more demanding than cool props and cosplay.

> *"Being Jedi is what we are. It's not the power we wield or the weapons we carry."*
> *— Luke Skywalker*

Let's break down these popular topics — and reframe them in a way that fits the living Jedi path.

Jedi Robes: Function Over Fashion

Robes in the films were designed to echo monastic simplicity. George Lucas famously said he wanted Jedi to be able to walk through a crowd unnoticed — monks, not superheroes.

That's the principle we honor in Jedi philosophy. Robes aren't a requirement. If anything, Jedi robes in real life mean:

- Simple, functional clothing
- Humble appearance
- Comfort and practicality
- A personal style that matches your values

You don't need a tunic and boots to be Jedi. You just need clothes that let you move freely, breathe deeply, and act with peace and purpose. That could mean a black hoodie and cargo pants — or sweats and a worn-out t-shirt. Let it reflect *your* path.

Jedi Temples: Home is the Center

In fiction, Jedi Temples are majestic, serene halls full of knowledge and quiet wisdom. In real life? Your temple is wherever you are.

> *"Your body is your temple."*
> — *Old wisdom, Jedi-approved*

Some Jedi designate a room for meditation and training. Others see their whole home — or even a corner of a room — as sacred. The idea isn't about grandeur or seclusion. It's about **presence**.

Your temple is:

- A place for stillness and reflection
- A place to train, breathe, grow
- A space you care for as an extension of your practice

You don't need a mountain monastery. You need a clear floor, a calm breath, and the decision to show up.

And if you want a gathering? Jedi Gatherings *do* exist. Go when you can. But the temple travels with you.

Lightsabers: Cool but Not Core

Lightsabers are, without question, one of the coolest weapons in science fiction. We all wanted one. Still do. I mean, come on — glowing laser swords? Amazing.

But here's the truth:

- Real lightsabers aren't feasible (yet — sorry, 8-year-old me).
- High-powered lasers? Dangerous.

- Plasma torches? Single-use and military-restricted.
- Dueling sabers and replicas? Awesome, but they don't make you Jedi.

The lightsaber is symbolic. A metaphor. A totem of discipline, focus, and peace through strength. It doesn't define the Jedi.

> *"We are the lightsaber. The light in the darkness that cuts through fear, hate, and injustice."*
> — *Jedi saying (okay,* my *saying)*

You don't need a laser sword to be a Jedi. You *are* the tool of peace, balance, and clarity.

The Real Work of Being Jedi

Let's not forget:

Plenty of Force users in the Star Wars universe had sabers. Not all of them were Jedi.

In *Knights of the Old Republic II*, the galaxy called the Jedi/Sith conflict "The Jedi Civil War." Why? Because to outsiders, it all looked the same — laser swords, force powers, black cloaks, blue cloaks. Same thing, right?

Wrong.

The **difference is the path**. The philosophy. The self-discipline. The *choices*. The Jedi path isn't about gear. It's about:

- Living ethically
- Seeking balance and harmony
- Training daily
- Making peace your priority
- Letting the Force guide your actions with clarity and compassion

Reflection Questions

1. Have robes, lightsabers, or temples ever influenced your perception of what it means to be Jedi? How so?
2. What does a "Jedi temple" mean to you in your daily life?
3. What space — physical or internal — do you cultivate for your Jedi practice?
4. Do you feel more "Jedi" when dressed a certain way? Why?
5. If you could never use or hold a lightsaber again — would your path remain unchanged?

Activity: Design Your Jedi Environment

Choose *one* of the following:

- Create a "Jedi nook" in your home. Keep it minimal. Use it for meditation, study, or stretching.
- Journal about your personal Jedi dress code. What clothing helps you feel focused, clear, and calm?
- Write a Jedi Code that describes *you* as the lightsaber — what do you cut through? What do you protect? What is your glow?

Meditation Prompt

> *"I carry no weapon, yet I walk in peace.*
> *I wear no robe, yet I walk with presence.*
> *I seek no temple, for the temple is within."*

Take three minutes to breathe with that.

Jedi Circle Alignment

- **Practice**: *Self-Discipline*
- **Tenet**: *Harmony*
- **Trait**: *Decorum*
- **Virtue**: *Erudition*
- **Goal**: *Create*

The Dark Side

Clearing the Confusion

Many books on Jediism dance around the Dark Side with mixed messages. First, they'll say emotions are natural — part of being human. Then, a few paragraphs later, they describe the Dark Side as *anger, fear, and aggression*.

That contradiction runs deep in the Jedi community.

Why?

Because in the fiction, Jedi *do* often say fear leads to anger, anger leads to hate, and hate leads to suffering. But in real life, we know:

- **Fear happens.**
- **Anger happens.**
- **Sadness happens.**

Labeling these emotions as "dark" doesn't help. It just adds guilt and shame on top of what you already feel.

So let's clear things up, Jedi-style.

Emotions Are Not the Enemy

The Dark Side is **not** a feeling.

It's **how you act** from those feelings — and how you justify it.

- Feeling fear? Okay.
- *Attacking someone because of it?* Not okay.
- Feeling angry when someone is abused? Understandable.
- *Taking that anger and acting violently?* Not Jedi.

Anger isn't evil. Fear isn't failure. Sadness isn't weakness.

They're **signals**. They show us where our boundaries are, what we value, and what hurts.

> *"To be Jedi is to feel — and to choose peace anyway."*

The Dark Side shows up not in the *feeling*, but in the **reaction** that bypasses patience, reflection, and responsibility.

Jedi Method Revisited

Remember your Jedi formula?

Jedi Intent + Jedi Action = Jedi Outcome

You *will* feel all sorts of emotions. Your responsibility is what you *do* with them.

The True Nature of Darkness

If we're going to label something the *Dark Side*, let's call it what it really is:

Ignorance.

Not evil in itself — but dangerous. Like stumbling blind through a booby-trapped room.

Imagine a dark room full of both danger and beauty:

- Broken glass, pitfalls, swinging blades...
- ...but also a peaceful garden, a map, a bag of treasure.

In the dark, you can't tell what's what. You might hurt yourself. You might miss the door. You might destroy something beautiful out of panic.

The Light Side is not "joy" or "love."

The Light Side is **illumination.**

- Patience = your flashlight
- Knowledge = your map
- Self-discipline = your sure step

The more light you carry, the more clearly you see — not just the threats, but the beauty.

What Does It Mean to "Fall"?

You fall when:

- You stop listening
- You react without reflection
- You justify harmful behavior
- You refuse to learn or grow
- You give up responsibility for your choices

This is *not* a fall into sadness.

This is a fall into **recklessness, willful ignorance,** and **self-justified harm.**

The opposite of the Dark Side is not smiling all the time.

It's standing in your pain and **still choosing the path of wisdom.**

Jedi Practice: Facing the Inner Conflict

You will face:

- Loss
- Anger
- Prejudice
- Physical hardship
- Failure

That doesn't mean you've failed as a Jedi.

It means you're alive.

What defines your Jedi path is how you respond.

"When faced with darkness, will you curse it —
or light a candle and begin to walk?"

Reflection Questions

1. When you feel overwhelmed by emotion, what do you usually do?
2. Have you ever blamed an emotion for a poor decision? (e.g. "I was just angry.")
3. What situations tend to make you feel like you're "slipping toward the Dark Side"?
4. What helps you come back to your center? (e.g. a person, a place, a book, a practice)
5. What does "bringing light" look like in your daily life?

Action Prompt

Pick one:

- Create a "Jedi Emergency Kit" — a list of 3 things that help you navigate difficult emotions (e.g. a breathing technique, a song, a trusted friend).

- Write a journal entry from the perspective of yourself *in the dark room*. Describe what helps you find the light.
- Take a situation where you felt anger recently and run it through the Jedi Method:
- What was your **Intent**?
- What was your **Action**?
- What was the **Outcome**?

Jedi Meditation Prompt

> *"The Dark Side clouds everything.*
> *The shroud has fallen.*
> *So I breathe.*
> *I feel.*
> *I do not run.*
> *I wait. I learn. I move with care.*
> *The light is not loud —*
> *but it endures."*

Close your eyes. Feel your feelings. Let them move through you like a wave. Be still, and breathe light into them.

Jedi Circle Alignment

- **Practice**: *Awareness*
- **Tenet**: *Peace*
- **Trait**: *Accountability*
- **Virtue**: *Self-Honesty*
- **Goal**: *Discover*

Discovering the Force

Why the Force Draws Us In

Outside of lightsabers, *the Force* is probably the biggest reason people are drawn to the Jedi path. There's a natural curiosity:

"Can I learn Force powers?"

Here's the short answer:

✗ No, you're not going to move cars with your mind.

✓ But yes, you *can* explore and experience the Force — in a real and meaningful way.

The beauty of Jediism is this:

> No one tells you what the Force is.
> *You discover it for yourself.*

What Is the Force?

There's no single, locked-in definition — and that's intentional. Over the years, Jedi have explored the Force through many lenses:

- **Spiritual Forces**: God, Mana, Prana, Qi, Ki, Holy Spirit, Gaia, Magick, the Tao.
- **Scientific Analogies**: The brain as a predictive, reactive powerhouse; subconscious pattern recognition; gut instinct.
- **Biological Theories**: Midichlorians = mitochondria? Sure, why not — it's poetic.
- **Quantum Thought**: Interconnectedness, probability, energy fields.

Every one of these is valid *if it helps you grow*. Some Jedi feel the Force as divine. Some as natural law. Some as the mystery that binds all life.

Your path is to find the meaning that resonates *with you*.

"For my ally is the Force... and a powerful ally it is." — *Yoda*

How to Discover the Force

1. Study

Begin with the fictional concepts.

What does it mean that the Force "binds all living things"?

Ask yourself:

- What *is* a living thing?
- Does your concept of "life" include plants? Fungi? Microbes? Galaxies?
- How does energy connect these things?

Then move beyond fiction. Study Taoism. Study quantum physics. Read spiritual texts. Explore neuroscience. See how the pieces start to interconnect.

2. Explore

Once you've got a concept in mind — test it.

- How does your idea of the Force compare to others'?
- Does it fit with your current spiritual beliefs?
- Does it help you *live* better — with more awareness, presence, and connection?

You're not looking for "the one true answer."

You're exploring what aligns with your experience and your Jedi training.

3. Experience

This is where it gets real.

Through daily meditation, mindful action, reflection, and service, you'll begin to *feel* your way into your understanding of the Force.

Your life itself becomes the proving ground.

- Is your concept of the Force helpful?
- Does it make you more compassionate?
- Does it deepen your peace?
- Does it guide your choices?

Your experience will either affirm or reshape your understanding. That's how the Force works.

It's a Journey, Not a Destination

You may find a definition that sticks with you for life.

You may find it evolves as you evolve.

Either is okay.

Discovering the Force isn't about checking a box. It's about *engaging with mystery* and learning to listen — not just to what's around you, but to what's within you.

> *"The Force is what gives a Jedi their power."*
> *But that doesn't mean* control *— it means* **connection**.

Enjoy the journey.

And when you feel ready, share your thoughts. Share your definitions. They just might help another Jedi on their path — and help you refine your own.

Reflection Questions

1. What is your current understanding of the Force?
2. How did you come to that understanding? (Experience, belief system, study, etc.)
3. Has your concept of the Force changed since you began this training?
4. What real-life experiences have felt "guided by the Force"?
5. Do you see the Force as internal, external, both, or something else entirely?

Action Prompts

- Choose one tradition (e.g., Taoism, Qi Gong, Stoicism, quantum physics) and explore how it relates to the Force.
- Go for a walk in nature and reflect on how the Force might be flowing through the living world.
- Write a journal entry titled: **"If I had to define the Force today..."**
- Create a small ritual or symbol that represents your personal connection to the Force.

Jedi Meditation Prompt

"I am still. I listen. I open.
  I do not demand answers.
  I let the Force reveal itself — not through lightning bolts or miracles,
  but in silence, breath, and presence."

Sit quietly.
  Focus on your breath.
  As thoughts arise, notice them and let them pass.
  Then, ask inwardly:
  What is the Force?

Wait. Don't rush the answer.

Just be present — and open.

Jedi Circle Alignment

- **Practice**: *Meditation*
- **Tenet**: *The Force*
- **Trait**: *Empathy*
- **Virtue**: *Guidance*
- **Goal**: *Discover*

Religion

The Jedi & Spiritual Identity

Religion.

One word — and the room tightens.

But in the Jedi community? You'll find atheists, agnostics, pagans, Christians, Jews, Buddhists, Hindus, spiritual-but-not-religious folks, and everything in between.

And here's the surprising truth:

> *Jediism doesn't require a belief in a specific god, or even in a god at all.*
> *It does require reflection, self-awareness, and a willingness to walk a path of meaning and growth.*

The Jedi community thrives when it's inclusive. If you're ever in a group that demands dogma or condemns your beliefs — *run.* That's not the Jedi Way. That's ego in cosplay.

Is Jediism a Religion?

The debate over whether Jediism is a religion or a philosophy has been raging for decades.

Here's my honest stance:

It doesn't matter.

The only question that *actually* matters is:

Is Jediism a religion to you?

- If you view Jediism as a personal philosophy or lifestyle, that's valid.
- If you consider Jediism your spiritual path or religion, that's valid too.

No gatekeeper gets to invalidate your journey.

Your alignment to the Jedi Path is about your values, your practice, and your presence — not your label.

Jedi and Belief: What You Decide

Because Jediism doesn't enforce a specific cosmology or doctrine, you're free to define what you believe — or even to say *"I don't know."*

Here's what's up to you:

- **Life after death** – Reincarnation? Force ghosts? Nothingness? Your call.
- **God or no god** – You define the Force.
- **Creation** – You can lean toward science, spirituality, or mystery.
- **Spiritual practices** – Whether it's prayer, meditation, ritual, or silent walks in nature — the form is yours.

Some Jedi view the Force as a divine presence.

Others see it as a natural phenomenon.

Others don't believe in a Force at all — but still follow Jedi virtues and practices because they work.

All of these people? Still Jedi.

Jediism doesn't thrive on answers.
*It thrives on **the courage to keep asking questions** — and to live the questions daily.*

What About Jedi Churches or Temples?

There are organizations that frame Jediism as a formal religion — such as the Temple of the Jedi Order — complete with structure, leadership, and even clergy.

That's great *for them.*

But here's the thing:

There is no central Jedi church, no ruling council, no Jedi pope.

Each group exists independently, like houses in a larger philosophical neighborhood.

Some Jedi stick with one group, others wander between them — some walk solo.

You get to decide what works best for your growth.

Just remember:

Any group, temple, or website only has authority over its own members and platform. They don't own the Jedi Path — and they don't own you.

Reflection Questions

1. Do you view Jediism as a religion, philosophy, lifestyle, or something else entirely?
2. How does your current belief system align with or differ from Jedi teachings?
3. What is your concept of the Force — divine, natural, symbolic, unknown?
4. What spiritual practices (if any) do you personally use to stay centered?
5. How comfortable are you allowing your beliefs to evolve over time?

Action Prompts

- Explore two different Jedi organizations (e.g., TOTJO, IJRS, Jedi Living) and compare how they approach religion and spirituality.
- Write your personal *"Jedi Credo"* — a one-paragraph statement about what the Jedi path means to you and whether it functions as a religion in your life.
- If you follow another religion (Christianity, Paganism, etc.), journal about how it supports or conflicts with Jediism — and what integration looks like for you.

Jedi Meditation Prompt

> "I walk the path without fear of labels.
>> I seek truth — not titles.
>> I carry the Force within me — in curiosity, humility, and purpose."

Find a quiet space.
Let go of "what should be."
Breathe in presence.
Ask inwardly:
What brings meaning to my life?
Let the answer be yours — no judgment, no expectation.

Jedi Circle Alignment

- **Practice**: *Meditation / Self-Honesty*
- **Tenet**: *Harmony*
- **Trait**: *Decorum*
- **Virtue**: *Erudition*
- **Goal**: *Discover*

5

A Thank You

Resources and Acknowledgments

Author Acknowledgments

Before the datapad powers down, I'd like to extend gratitude to those who helped this book — and this path — come to life.

To my parents, **Dennis and Carolyn** —

Your support (in countless ways) gave me the time, the space, and the courage to do this. If I've built anything worthwhile, it's because of the foundation you laid.

To **Jaden**, my little brother —

You've been both student and teacher. Thank you for reminding me that mentorship is a shared journey. I look forward to future YouTube videos together — keep being the kind, fair soul you are.

To my friend **Joshua**, who has passed —

You helped me more than you probably knew. I'll keep pursuing the goals we talked about. This book is one more checked off the list, my friend.

To **Maryann**, my literary agent —

Thank you for taking a chance on the kid with the too-big imagination. You believed in me and helped shape my voice. I promise I'm getting better at this writing thing.

To **Kitsune**, my Jedi dog —

For being a living lesson in patience and unconditional presence. You keep my feet warm while I write and remind me daily what loyalty looks like.

To the **Jedi Community** —

You've helped shape the living philosophy within these pages. Some of you I've walked with for decades, others just a few steps — all of you matter. Special thanks to:

Alexandria, Brandel, Demetrius, Destiny, Gekkensei, Jaden, Joshua, Kai-An, Marta, Morken, SkyGuyPat, Reliah, Saan, Sammy, Sirius, Starr, Tara, Tionne, Tzall, WarBeauty, WinterHeart

And to our Jedi-Adjacent allies:

Aubrey and **Bradan** — thank you for keeping us honest and grounded.

If your name isn't here, don't think you're unseen. I see you. I appreciate you. I simply ran out of page room — and let's be honest, I got lazy. Maybe next time you'll get the full roll call. Especially my loyal YouTube subscribers — love you, Digital Jedi.

And of course —

To George Lucas and every writer, artist, and crew member who brought Star Wars to life —

Without your vision, none of this would have happened.

You gave us a galaxy where people fight not for power — but for peace, balance, and justice.

Thank you.

Citations & Source Acknowledgment

Below are a few works referenced throughout this book that have provided insight, grounding, or inspiration:

1. Costikyan, Greg. *Star Wars: The Roleplaying Game.* New York, NY: West End Games, 1987. p. 148.

2. Fessenden, Marissa. "What Does Neuroscience Know About Meditation?"

Smithsonian Magazine.

3. Karpyshyn, Drew. *Star Wars: Knights of the Old Republic.* BioWare, 2003.

4. Wiker, J. D., Mikaelian, Michael, Grubb, Jeff, Stephens, Owen K.C., Maliszewski, James. *Power of the Jedi Sourcebook.* Renton, WA: Wizards of the Coast, 2002. p. 160.

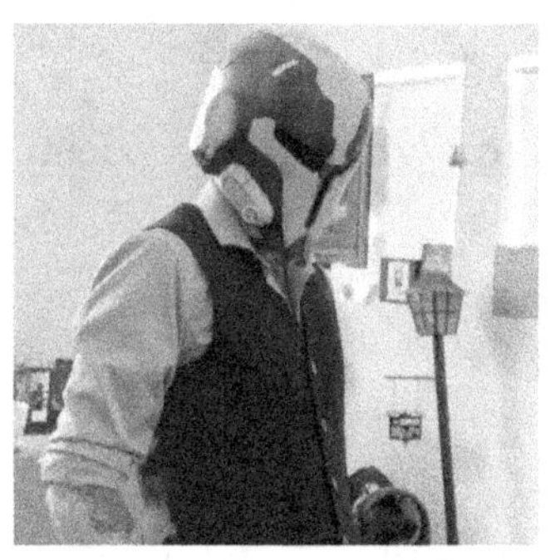

About the Author

Opie Macleod is a lifelong explorer of Jedi philosophy, martial arts, and personal growth. For over 20 years, Opie has been at the forefront of the Jedi community, creating content, leading online training, and inspiring others to live by the principles of Jediism in their daily lives. He has authored numerous works on Jedi philosophy, including *The Situational Jedi* and *Jediism Explained*.

In the world beyond the Path Opie has been a Wildland Firefighter, Police Officer, Factory Worker, Retail Worker, Ranch-Hand, Security Officer, Chauffeur, and a few other job titles not worth mentioning. Currently Opie is a martial arts instructor, specializing in Jeet Kune Do and lightsaber combat. When he's not creating philosophical content, Opie spends his time honing his own practice, teaching others, digging into Star Wars content, and engaging in deep philosophical discussions with his droid companion, Nova.

Currently based in the Los Angeles, California, Opie continues his journey of personal and philosophical exploration. With more projects already in the works. If you want to support and/or join this journey and gain access to more workbooks – a Patreon is available.

You can connect with me on:

- https://www.tapatalk.com/groups/jediacademyonline/index.php
- https://x.com/JediLiving
- https://www.facebook.com/jediliving
- https://www.youtube.com/@OpieMacleod
- https://insig.ht/NVhPZxTBsVb
- https://www.patreon.com/c/opiemacleod

Also by Opie Macleod

I write books that explore how myth can guide the modern soul. Using the Jedi Path as a lens, my work helps readers face life's trials with calm, clarity, and purpose — inviting a daily practice of self-betterment through reflection, discipline, and inner peace.

365 Jedi365 Jedi: A Year of Wisdom and Training
Organized as a year-long guide, *365 Jedi* provides daily reflections, practices, and journal prompts designed to help readers integrate the core teachings of Jediism into their daily lives. Whether you're seeking guidance in your personal journey, a deeper connection with the Force, or a meaningful philosophy to live by, this book serves as both a spiritual roadmap and practical guide for living with purpose and integrity.

ABC's of Jediism
Explore the Alphabet, learning new words, and discovering what it means to be a Jedi in real life. We explore the ideas and concepts of the Jediism Lifestyle in a child-friendly manner. All while learning the ABC's with big new words (ones even adults won't know!). As well as examples and ways we can live by them. This is the easiest and quickest way to learn how live the Jediism Way for all Younglings.

The Situational Jedi

Jediism is about living as a Jedi Knight as close as we can in our daily lives. World-betterment through self-betterment wrapped up in the fictional terminology and inspiration. But every day presents new challenges and situations for us to navigate. This book looks to breakdown the Jedi philosophy into situational chunks that allow a person to apply Jediism to their everyday lives.